Drawing Conclusions on Henry Ford

Drawing Conclusions on Henry Ford

Rudolph Alvarado and Sonya Alvarado

Ann Arbor

THE UNIVERSITY OF MICHIGAN PRESS

Copyright © by the University of Michigan 2001

Published in the United States of America by
The University of Michigan Press
Manufactured in the United States of America
∞ Printed on acid-free paper

2004   2003   2002   2001   4   3   2   1

A CIP catalog record for this book is available from the British Library.

Library of Congress Cataloging-in-Publication Data

Alvarado, Rudolph.
   Drawing conclusions on Henry Ford / Rudolph Alvarado and Sonya
Alvarado.
      p.   cm.
   Includes index.
   ISBN 0-472-09766-0 — ISBN 0-472-06766-4
   1. Ford, Henry, 1863–1947.   2. Ford Motor Company—History. 3.
Automobile industry and trade—History.   4. Industrialists—United
States—Biography.   I. Alvarado, Sonya.   II. Title.

   HD9710.U54 F5335   2001
   338.7'6292'092—dc21   00-012898

For
Nichole Carole
Nathaniel Christian
Nicho Courtland
Natalio Cuyler
Daniel and Susanne Taylor

Acknowledgments

WE WOULD LIKE TO RECOGNIZE the staff at the Research Library of the Henry Ford Museum and Greenfield Village, especially Linda Skolarus, Romie Minor, and Patricia Orr. We also want to acknowledge Dr. David L. Lewis and Ford Bryan for their support in making this book a reality. A special thanks goes to the following libraries and newspapers: Ford Motor Company Archives; Library of Congress; State of Michigan Library; University of Michigan Graduate Library; Eastern Michigan University Library; Wayne State University Library; Detroit Public Library; New York Public Library; *Pittsburgh Post-Gazette; Chicago Daily Tribune; Detroit News; Detroit Free Press; Dallas Morning News; Des Moines Register;* and the *Dayton Daily News*. Without the contributions of these institutions, many of the prized cartoons featured here would have remained hidden from the public. A special thanks also goes to our editor at the University of Michigan Press, Mary Erwin, who provided encouragement, assistance, and advice throughout this project, and to the staff of the University of Michigan Press, for their hard work and contributions toward making this project a success.

Finally, we offer a special thanks and kiss to our daughter—and future Notre Dame graduate—Nichole Carole, who researched countless newspapers, magazines, and other sources for cartoons and articles. We also offer special thanks to our sons, Nathaniel, Nicho, and Natalio for their understanding and patience while we were working on this book.

Contents

Introduction

HENRY FORD BEGAN HIS LIFE as a farm boy in the wilderness of southeastern Michigan. He ended it as one of the richest men in the world. During this incredible journey, America and the rest of the world not only came to know Ford through numerous newspaper and magazine articles, biographies, and autobiographies, but they also came to know him through cartoons from a variety of genres. Many people who met Henry Ford in this way could barely read. It was not a skill in great demand at the turn of the century, especially in rural America. However, these same people could and did understand the cartoons that captured every major event of the auto baron's life. From his beginnings as a farm boy to his run for the presidency, cartoonists inked out a vivid picture of this man, sometimes critical, sometimes adulatory, but never indifferent. The drawings helped in creating the myth of this complex and enterprising man from America's industrial past.

Cartoons, or drawings that make a statement, are familiar elements of most modern newspapers. The biting wit and bold caricatures make the reader laugh at first, but, more important, these drawings make statements about current events, issues, and ultimately the people behind these events. Usually critical and often unflattering in nature, the political or editorial cartoon creates an admittedly one-sided yet extremely influential view of the events of the day. Today it is hard for any citizen of America to remember Richard Nixon as anything but the "Tricky Dick" emerging from the editorial pages of the 1970s. This ability of cartoons to shape and/or reshape the readership's way of viewing an event or a person makes these ephemeral art pieces important historical objects in their own right. Furthermore, examining this powerful medium through which a public figure like Henry Ford became familiar to the masses lets the modern reader understand how this subjective yet influential source of information helped create the popular myths of the man that still exist today.

Cartoons involving Henry Ford come from a variety of sources. Some are found in the Ford Motor Company's *Ford Times* and others on postcards or in specialty magazines, such as *Antique Automobiles*. The bulk of these cartoons, however, can be found in the newspapers of the time.

A history of the political and editorial cartoon demonstrates how significant this medium can be. Political and editorial cartoons, especially those featuring caricatures, are not a new phenomenon. Art historians trace the history of these cartoons as far back as the Roman Empire. In Pompeii archaeologists found a very unflattering portrait of a Roman centurion drawn by one of the soldiers in an army barracks. This picture with its exaggerated and distorted features obviously ridicules a forgotten officer. Some scholars search back even further, to Egypt, for evidence of humanity drawing authority figures with irreverence in order to make a statement. Certain unflattering sketches on King Tutankhamen's tomb proved to be portraits of his father-in-law. Art historians date the beginnings of the modern day political and editorial cartoons to eighteenth-century English cartoonist William Hogarth, who sketched a series of cartoon commentaries on English society of the time. Hogarth's style of gently ridiculing the gentry remained popular well into the nineteenth century.

The first American accredited with the drawing of a political cartoon is one of our founders, Benjamin Franklin. Franklin was not only the first American political and editorial cartoonist, he was also one of the first public figures in America to be caricatured by cartoonists. The first cartoon that Franklin drew, in 1754, depicted a serpent divided into eight parts with the caption "JOIN, or DIE." Franklin presented the cartoon at the Albany congress as a visual demonstration of why the colonies needed to form a union. Franklin's divided snake appeared throughout the Revolutionary War as a powerful symbol of the colonies in cartoons on both the British and the American sides. After the Revolution, political and editorial cartoons appeared periodically in newspapers and magazines. By the time of the American Civil War, several

This serpent figure appeared on the masthead of the *Massachusetts Spy* in 1774 with the engraving "Join, or Die" underneath it. A point of interest is that Paul Revere was the engraver.

artists had made a name for themselves as political cartoonists. Yet these cartoons were not regular features, especially in newspaper format, because of the expense of printing them.

One of the most famous events surrounding a political cartoon happened on July 1, 1876, when the young cartoonist Thomas Nast pictured William Marcy Tweed, the infamous New York political boss, in a prison suit holding two orphans by their collars. The cartoon ran in the popular *Harper's Weekly* magazine. Nast was trying to make the point that Boss Tweed's political machine was putting the homeless and helpless in jail while the real criminals were running free around the city of New York. Thomas Nast proceeded to run a series of cartoons on Boss Tweed that ultimately brought down the crooked Tammany Hall institution. While it was well known throughout New York that Tweed and his cronies were corrupt politicians, little could be done about them until the Nast campaign ignited the passions of the largely migrant population of New York's slums into action. Ultimately Tweed fled to Spain with the prison cartoon stashed away in his pocket. When he arrived in Spain it was mistaken for a wanted poster. Tweed landed in jail. Concerning Nast's cartoons, Tweed demanded of his employees, "Stop them damn pictures! I don't care so much what the papers write about me. My constituents can't read. But, damn it, they can see pictures."

The explosive growth of political and editorial cartoons in newspapers during the late 1800s owes most of its success to technology. New technology during this time allowed newspapers to print cartoons on a daily basis rather than the biweekly or monthly cartoon. Before that time both expense and technical difficulties prevented cartoons from becoming a regular feature. Cartoons also could be only the size of the narrow columns of the press.

One small but significant banquet in 1884 greatly influenced the growth of the popularity of political cartoons. Joseph Pulitzer printed a cartoon called "The Royal Feast of Belshazzar Blaine and the Money Kings" as a comment on a dinner held in honor of the Republican candidate for president, James Blain. The cartoon created a great stir since it showed Blaine living it up at an opulent banquet with the robber barons of the country. The Democrats made sure that this image appeared on billboards and in pamphlets in the hands of all the right people. Since Blain lost several hundred votes in pivotal New York State, this cartoon is now acknowledged to have helped put Grover Cleveland in the White House. Soon after this event, most major newspapers within the United States felt it necessary to have a political cartoon in each edition. These cartoons came to be expected by the American public, and people looked to them for information about what was going on in the world.

Not only were politicians the targets for these cartoons; industrialists, capitalists, and inventors became prime targets as well. Men such as J. D. Rockefeller, William R. Hearst, J. P. Morgan, and even the auto magnate Henry Ford became the subjects of these cartoons.

The cartoons collected in this volume are representative of hundreds of cartoons depicting the many ventures of Henry Ford

Vol. XX.—No. 1018.] NEW YORK, SATURDAY, JULY 1, 1876. [WITH A SUPPLEMENT.
PRICE TEN CENTS.

Entered according to Act of Congress, in the Year 1876, by Harper & Brothers, in the Office of the Librarian of Congress, at Washington.

TWEED-LE-DEE AND TILDEN-DUM.

REFORM TWEED. "If all the people want is to have somebody arrested, I'll have you plunderers convicted. You will be allowed to escape; nobody will be hurt; and then TILDEN will go to the White House, and I to Albany as Governor."

The cartoon that sent Tweed to prison. (From *Harper's Weekly,* July 1, 1876.)

the automaker, capitalist, social reformer, pacifist, and politician. Each chapter focuses on a significant event in Ford's life and the relevant cartoons that accompanied the time period. Chapter 1 looks specifically at that revolutionary invention of Henry's, the Model T, more affectionately known as the "Tin Lizzie." The cartoons in this chapter capture the affection the average person had for the Model T as well as the progressive pairing of Henry with his car so that the two almost became one and the same in people's minds. Chapter 2 examines the portrayal in the popular press of Ford's innovative five-dollar day. These cartoons let us see the maverick automaker taking on the very industry he helped create in order to boost production and help his workers at the same time. We see the hopes of the masses on one side and the jeers of the moneymakers on the other in these cartoons. Chapter 3 deals with Henry Ford's failed attempts to bring peace to Europe during 1915 by way of a chartered ship full of idealistic delegates for peace from the United States. This series of cartoons demonstrates a change from affectionate humor to biting sarcasm on the part of many cartoonists. Historians mark this event as the first major disappointment of Ford's public life. Before he sailed on this ship for

Europe, he was the darling of industrial America, the one manufacturer who cared about the average citizens and their desires. Afterward his simplistic ideas became the fodder for cartoonists' lampoons. Chapter 4 covers Ford's run for the U.S. Senate in Michigan and the grassroots efforts to get him to run for president between 1916 and 1920. These bids were never taken seriously by Ford, who was too busy defending his decision to cut the dividend payments of stockholders to a minimum in order to finance his expansion of the Highland Park plant and the building of a blast furnace and foundry at a new location on the Rouge River. Stockholders John F. and Horace Dodge had filed a lawsuit and obtained a restraining order freezing company funds targeted for this expansion effort. However, even with Ford ignoring the call to office, the efforts of the public proved fruitful for cartoonists wanting to make a point about the state of the union. In chapter 5 the cartoons show Ford once again being called to serve the public in the capacity of president. In this presidential race of 1924, people other than the farmers began to view Ford as a real prospect for the presidency. With a corrupt Harding on the GOP ticket and no strong Democratic prospects, Ford and his car appear in cartoons as an independent force puttering closer and closer to the White House. Chapter 6 covers the cartoonists' depiction of Ford's proposed purchase of Muscle Shoals, deemed an effort to aid American farmers. Ford gave up his run for the presidency for a chance of securing this property. By the end of this venture, Ford had not only lost the respect of many a farmer, he had also lost in his efforts to build his dream city on the shores of Muscle Shoals. Chapter 7 describes the launching of Ford's attack on the Jewish people in a series of articles for his own *Dearborn Independent*. Started in 1920, this attack would last until 1927, when Ford settled a lawsuit with a prominent Chicago attorney, Aaron Sapiro. Cartoons at this time covered the Sapiro lawsuit and mocked the fact that Ford claimed he had never read the articles concerning Jews in his newspaper. Chapter 8 discusses the ending of the era of the Model T, which occurred when Ford decided that the time was right to introduce the Model A. In this chapter, Ford is seen playing a variety of roles from mother hen to doting father as he prepares to give birth to the Model A. The pressure was tremendous, and expectations were high, as people wondered if Ford would succeed in replacing the legendary Model T. As the world pondered this question, Ford's prejudicial articles regarding the Jewish people were quickly forgotten. In the concluding chapter, an examination of Ford's feelings and thoughts on cartoons is undertaken, and a conclusion is drawn as to the part cartoons played in establishing the Ford legend.

The selected cartoons featured here represent the first full-scale study of Ford's evolutionary portrayal in cartoons relating to major events in his life. Together these images offer a fresh perspective on the history of Henry Ford. In their own time these cartoons helped to shape public opinion by capturing an idea in a single, simple image. This allowed an argument to be understood in an instant, thus reaching an audience that might have been lost with the written or spoken word. For today's readers, these cartoons offer more than a simple message. While historians are limited to presenting the straight facts, the cartoons force the reader to come to their own conclusions about the facts on Henry Ford through the use of humor, sarcasm, irony, exaggeration, and ridicule. They serve to introduce Ford to a new generation, and they add yet another layer of knowledge and information to the established Ford canon.

CHAPTER 1

The Car That Made the Man:
Henry Ford's Model T

HENRY FORD HAD A DREAM. He wanted to "build a motor car for the great multitude" so low in price that a man making a decent salary would be able to purchase one.[1] The Model T was the fulfillment of that dream. Today, people find it hard to understand the significance of Henry Ford's car to the average person in the early decades of the twentieth century. On almost any street in America today, several automobiles line the curbs and driveways. Car dealerships take up city blocks, and the makes, models, colors, and sizes are endless. The modern commuter traveling thirty miles a day to work or a person traveling a few hundred miles to visit a relative is common. The automobile made this lifestyle possible for millions of people starting with the Model T. The importance of this car cannot be exaggerated. Even as the century drew to an end, *Time Magazine* named the Model T the "automobile that defined the twentieth century from start to finish."[2] The ranking was based on the Model T's "single design, and inexpensive, mass-produced parts," which made the "pioneering vehicle affordable to millions."[3] It was the vehicle that made Ford Motor Company a household word across America and throughout the world. This recognition was also the reason why early cartoons concentrated on the Model T and not on Henry Ford.

In order to explain why this was the case, it is important to point out that at the time just before the Model T appeared on the scene a large portion of America's population lived in rural areas. At the beginning of this century, people were confined to the distance a horse and buggy could travel round trip in a day. That meant that a person's destination could be no more than twelve miles away from home if he or she did not plan to stay overnight. Because of this fact, most people in rural areas lived in isolation for

A Hustling Auto Salesman

Early cartoons centered around the Model T and not on Henry Ford. In this cartoon, C. B. McAllister, "a hustling auto salesman," proudly holds a Model T. In the article accompanying the cartoon, McAllister claimed that he was "the man who put the 'Ford' in afford." The trademark of the winged pyramid on the side of the garage with the scripted Ford name inside was introduced in 1912 by Glen Buck, the first editor of the *Ford Times,* a magazine for customers. Of the trademark, Buck said that it "was a happy combination of two of the oldest Egyptian symbols—the pyramid symbolizing strength and stability— the scarab wings symbolizing lightness and grace," (*Ford Times,* March 1912, back cover). The words "The Universal Car," which cannot be seen in the cartoon, appeared directly under the Ford name. (From *Washington Rebuttal,* Washington, Pennsylvania, ca. 1914.)

most of the year. Farmers rarely traveled outside the boundaries of their land except to bring a crop to the market or to buy supplies once every few months or even once a year. Automobiles and especially the Model T erased this way of life forever.

Henry Ford's Model T arrived on the market October 1, 1908. The popularity of the "Tin Lizzie," as the car was affectionately

Each Model T sold helped to build the car's reputation as a dependable and durable means of transportation and also added to its reputation for affordability. In this cartoon, "Old Sport" dreams of the day when he can retire after his owner purchases a Ford. Note that the scripted "Ford" name at the bottom of Old Sport's hat was a Ford Motor Company trademark dating back to Ford's first plant located on Mack Avenue in Detroit. The trademark was designed by C. Harold Willis and was not meant to be a facsimile of Henry Ford's handwriting. (From *Ford Times*, Detroit, Michigan, ca. 1914.)

known, grew so quickly that the factory could not keep up with orders. Because of this demand, it was hard to ignore the growing phenomenon of the Model T and the changes it meant for the world's citizens. Once on the road, the Model T became an instant cultural icon, and it was not long before illustrators began both lampooning and praising the appearance and the qualities for which the car was known.

Thanks to the production methods introduced at the Rouge River plant in Dearborn, Michigan, the Model T enjoyed rapid and enormous success because its price dropped in the years following its debut. Starting at $850 in 1908, the price of the basic touring car fell to $290 by 1927, the final year of its production. Thanks to the economically priced Model T that was designed primarily for farm and family use, by the 1920s it was rarely possible to find a farm where a horse did most of the hauling and plowing.

Rapid introduction into American life was also made possible because of the Tin Lizzie's endurance on roads that were deeply rutted or muddy. The Model T's high wheelbase and planetary transmission, along with its lightweight body, made of vanadium, allowed the Model T to get in and out of the most impossible areas with ease.

To assert its superiority Henry Ford and Model T owners entered the car in several endurance races. The Model T managed to beat out all of its foes and create quite a stir. For example, at the grueling Pikes Peak run of 1922, a Model T owner was actually ridiculed relentlessly before the race only to win it in the end. In addition to these races, Ford dealers created promotional stunts to demonstrate the agility of the Model T. One event had the dealer in Nashville driving his Model T up the state capitol steps.

Consumers, especially farmers, found that they not only could afford this car and travel almost anywhere in it but that they could also use the Model T as an indispensable tool for farm labor. Farmers hitched makeshift plows to the Model T and drove it through the fields or jacked up the backs of their vehicles and replaced a tire with a pulley to which was attached a belt that ran a piece of machinery. When these innovative uses of the Model T became well known, it did not take long for cartoonists to lampoon this utilitarian nature of the Tin Lizzie.

The feats farmers put the Model T through would have been impossible with the heavier and bulkier cars on the market at the time. When Ford Motor Company dealers promoted an automobile club that limited membership to owners of the Model T, they made sure to collect and exchange members' ideas concerning their use of a Model T. In turn this information was made available to potential customers, who, impressed with the many ways in which the car could be a resource in their daily lives, would then purchase their own Model T.

The idea for this 1918 editorial cartoon showing Ford and his Model T riding up
the steps of Capitol Hill was borrowed directly from a publicity stunt in which a
Ford dealer actually drove a Model T up the sixty-six steps of the Tennessee state
capitol in 1911. The stunt was only one of many in which Ford dealers drove a
Model T up courthouse steps or steep inclines. The artist of this cartoon apparently remembered the significance these stunts had for the public when he drew
this cartoon signifying that the Model T and Henry Ford did not follow the established rut in the political road. (From *Cedar Rapids Times*, Iowa, ca. 1918.)

Urban dwellers soon discovered the benefits of owning a
Model T as well. They could live further away from their place of
employment if they owned a reliable Tin Lizzie. Before the avail-
ability of cheap automobile transportation, urban dwellers often
lived within walking distance of their jobs. Trolleys made it possible to move some distance away, but a commuter's options were

A 1912 Ford Motor Company advertisement read "Farmers' dollars are big dollars—because they are hard earned dollars. It is because the American farmer is ever a careful and painstaking buyer that he is today the happy and proud possessor of more than half the Ford cars in existence." The utilitarian nature of the Model T is captured brilliantly in this postcard, which shows "Samanthy" using her Model T to wash dishes, do the laundry, churn butter, and rock the baby to sleep, as her husband waits his turn. The fact that the Model T was viewed as a farmer's car kept some of the city elite from purchasing the vehicle. (From Commercial Colortype Company, Chicago, Illinois, ca. 1915.)

still limited by the placement of the trolley lines and trolley schedules until the arrival of Ford's car for the masses.

As the Model T became commonplace, it was inevitable that the more humorous aspects of this automobile would become the target of entertainers, satirists, and even owners. The very nature of the Model T, with its chugging engine, rattling frame, and utilitarian looks, lent itself to jokes of all sorts. This entertainment found its way into vaudeville acts, joke books, films, songs, and postcards. Editorial cartoonists and illustrators joined in this newfound joke craze. These jokes mostly followed three themes, which sometimes converged. The first set of jokes made fun of the Model T's size and utilitarian appearance as well as the less than smooth

Why Mr. Commuter bought a Ford

In an attempt to capture the urban market, Ford Motor Company published cartoons that showcased the benefits of owning a Model T. The commuter in this cartoon waits in the pouring rain with pant legs rolled up and his office bag soaked. This would not leave a positive impression on the boss. After buying a Model T, commuters did not have to be at the mercy of the trolley. With a Model T, a commuter was free to come and go as he or she pleased. (From *Ford Times*, Detroit, Michigan, ca. 1914.)

ride experienced by passengers. References to the Model T being anything from a roller skate to a tin can to an insect of some sort were common.

The second category of jokes demonstrated how the Model T could outperform and outmaneuver many of the other cars of the time. Most Tin Lizzie owners easily understood the caption "If you own a Ford, the world laughs at you or with you."

The final theme focused on the Model T as a "smart" person's car. Looks and size were not important. A Model T's owner was thrifty and wise. Why drive an oversized, overpriced, gas-guzzling vehicle when you could drive a Model T? Besides, what other car could people trust to get them through a driving rainstorm or a blizzard except a Model T?

While most of the automotive industry was still making the giant gas-guzzlers for the elite, by the early 1920s things began to change. Manufacturers such as Oldsmobile and Hudson began offering cars priced under one thousand dollars. As the decade progressed more and more automobile manufacturers were introducing their own low priced cars with quieter engines and sleeker designs. Even so, the Tin Lizzie outsold all models put together for several more years, but this new competition was eating away at the Model T's market. Ford Motor Company established its name with the Model T, making it almost impossible to part with the car. Moreover, Ford biographer Robert Lacey observed that Henry Ford came to view the Model T as "central to his very identity," which made redesigning or even replacing the Model T impossible.[4] With time Henry Ford's love of the car and identification with it proved fatal to the Tin Lizzie. While other cars grew quieter and sleeker, the Lizzie puttered along loudly proclaiming its status as "the Universal Car." Jokes about the obsolete nature of the Model T became a final theme explored in cartoons. The Model T was not a car for high society. It was a car for the rural individual. As rural America became connected to the big city by paved highways, the Model T's ability to travel makeshift roads became unnecessary. The advent of several tractor companies, which included Ford's own Fordson company, also took away the Model T's agricultural responsibilities.

Throughout the long years of production Henry Ford resisted

According to David L. Lewis, a Ford scholar, in his *The Public Image of Henry Ford,* "Ford jokes were as much a part of everyday conversation as shop talk, sports gossip, or interest in the weather and were as commonly voiced over a glass of tea at a church social as over a glass of beer at a corner saloon." These jokes served to popularize the social inferiority of the Model T and of the people who owned them. Here are some examples."Why is a Ford like a bathtub? Because you hate to be seen in one." A Ford reportedly ran over a chicken, which got up saying, "Cheep, cheep, cheep." Henry Ford, when offered $1.50 after repairing a farmer's stalled car, refused, saying that he had all the money he wanted. "You're a liar," retorted the farmer, "because if you had plenty of money you'd take some of it and buy yourself an 'automobile.' " (From Commercial Colortype Company, Detroit, Michigan, ca. 1914.)

changing the Model T's basic design. He did not have to; the market did not call for it. The Model T stood alone, and Henry Ford followed quietly in its shadow. It was not until Henry Ford's five-dollar-a-day announcement in 1914 that the man Henry Ford stepped forward and took center stage. By the time the press was done with the five-dollar-a-day story, the world never again said the name Model T without including the name Henry Ford in the same sentence. The world would finally discover the origin of the Tin Lizzie's personality: it came from Henry Ford himself.

Cartoons like this one published by the Ford Motor Company balanced out cartoons that joked about the Model T and its owners by showing Ford owners as comfortable, sensible, and confident people. These cartoons made their point but never lost the sense of humor that made a cartoon popular with readers. It is interesting to point out that if the price were adjusted to today's economy, the first Model T would have cost $9,400. In 1994, a Ford Tempo retailed at just under $13,000, and the Ford Focus LX four door averages $11,500. (From *Ford Times,* Detroit, Michigan, ca. 1914.)

FARMER — "HUH! FELLER COME ALONG HERE 'BOUT AN HOUR AGO ALL RIGHT — WITH A 'FORD'."

Because the Model T was associated with farmers from the beginning, a farmer knew about a Model T's ability to get out of a muddy situation. If only the city folks could smarten up, the world would be a better place. (From *Ford Times,* Detroit, Michigan, ca. 1914.)

If you were high society and allowed the norm of the day to dictate your life, you drove a "ton" of a car. If you were sensible and your own person, you drove a Model T. As people came to know Henry Ford, they slowly realized that he personified this way of thinking. Henry Ford was his own man: he did things his way, or he did not do them at all. (From *Ford Times,* Detroit, Michigan, ca. 1914.)

The fellow in this Model T could have been Henry Ford himself. With 164,452 cars sold in 1913 alone, Ford was one of the richest men in the world. The following year would bring record sales and worldwide public recognition for Henry Ford following his announcement of the five-dollar day. (From *Ford Times*, Detroit, Michigan, ca. 1914.)

CHAPTER 2

The Raise Heard 'round the World: The Five-Dollar Day

IF THE MODEL T BROUGHT THE Ford Motor Company recognition and profits, the announcement on January 5, 1914, that Ford Motor Company would pay five dollars for an eight-hour shift brought Henry Ford worldwide fame and near sainthood status. It was publicity that had eluded Ford even though from 1910 onward Detroit newspapers had published a number of articles on his activities as a farmer, a philanthropist, an industrialist, and a citizen. Ford first received regional recognition in 1911 when he won the celebrated Seldon patent suit. In this legal battle Ford was able to prove that George B. Seldon's 1895 patent for a "road carriage," which Seldon never actually built, was not a legitimate claim. This led to the demise of the Association of Licensed Automobile Manufacturers who, up to that time, had monopolized the industry. Surprisingly, this noteworthy event did not gain Ford recognition from the national press. Locally Ford was no better known than other automobile manufacturers, such as Henry M. Leland and Ransom Eli Olds. Following the five-dollar announcement big business laughed at or criticized Ford, just as some car owners laughed at and criticized the Model T. Yet Ford, just like his car, drove right past the ridicule and laughed right back as he followed his own practical heart. Ford was not going to be a money greedy capitalist. He would strip his company of excess profits just as the Model T was stripped of any excess that would make it a gas-guzzling machine.

Because of Ford's lack of national exposure, reporters working on the five-dollar-a-day story were the first to depict Ford the man. These accounts, which were published in newspapers throughout the world, eventually evolved into the Ford legend. On covering the news of the five-dollar day, Garet Garret, a reporter for *Every-*

Following the announcement of Ford's five-dollar day on January 5, 1914, portraits such as this one were published with biographies of Henry Ford in magazines and newspapers all over the world. For some it was the first image they had ever seen of the automotive pioneer. Ford's habit of always wearing a suit and tie was a trademark from the beginning of his career. Cartoonists often stressed his lean physique and his perfect posture, especially when Ford was pictured standing up to big business or the government. The biographies that ran with the portraits set the tone, if not the entire framework, for the Ford legend that came after. (From *New York Times*, New York, 1914.)

body's Magazine, wrote "It was surprising how little the people of Detroit knew of Henry Ford. There was no accepted Ford legend. Fame and wealth had overtaken him too suddenly."[1] Allan Nevins and Frank E. Hill, two preeminent Ford scholars, reiterate this observation in their book *Ford: The Times, the Man, the Company*, noting that "down to the five-dollar announcement, Ford's reputation was restricted to southern Michigan and to industrial circles."[2] After the announcement, however, as noted by David L.

Lewis in his book *The Public Image of Henry Ford,* the conservative *New York Times* "ran thirty-five stories on Ford within ninety days of the profit-sharing announcements, and no fewer than fourteen magazines carried biographies of the manufacturer during 1914. Biographical sketches of Ford appeared in thousands of newspapers, frequently running under eight-column streamers and filling entire pages."[3] Early realistic penciled renderings of Ford accompanied these biographies, thus providing readers with their first glimpse of what Henry Ford looked like. It must be remembered that print media were the main source of information at this time. The motion picture industry was in its infancy, and television was still some years down the road. Thus published materials served as the public's only source of news and images of Henry Ford.

Why is the establishment of a Ford legend such a vital element in the history of Henry Ford as seen in cartoons? Cartoons, especially political and editorial cartoons, reflect the personalities and issues of the times. They are, by design, an exaggeration or a simplification of facts regarding the subject at hand. Points are made by placing an emphasis on a person's appearance or personality traits or on facts about the topic under consideration. Regardless of the point being stressed, the issue is easily recognized by the audience. This is accomplished by including in the cartoon objects or concepts that are familiar to the people. For this reason, cartoons lambasting or praising Ford would not have made an impact if the audience did not know enough about Ford's background, his professional philosophy, his physical appearance, or his personal beliefs and values to comprehend the implied meaning of a specific cartoon.

What made this particular scenario perfect for cartoonists was that biographies about Henry Ford gave them an opportunity to get to know Henry Ford at the same time their public was getting to know him. What they learned about Henry Ford was that he came from a farm; that he left home at sixteen; that he was a "tinkerer"; that he was his own man, self-taught; that he had earned everything he had on his own; that he did not have to step on anybody to make it to the top; that he was innovative; that there was nothing he could not do if he put his mind, and money, to it.

Finally, and most important, they learned that Ford was always an underdog fighting for the good of humankind, just as the Model T was an underdog. Ask someone today to tell you about Henry Ford, and he or she may be apt to repeat information found in a *New York Times* advertisement that publicized the newspaper's biography of Henry Ford. In the advertisement, which ran on January 9, 1914, Henry Ford was described as a

> farmer boy who had a bent for mechanics; now a tall, slender man of fifty, throbbing with energy, radiating hope, a fighter of monopoly, a lover of birds and flowers and of the simple life. This is HENRY FORD, a man whose net profits last year make it possible for him this year to put $10,000,000 extra into the pay envelopes of his employes [*sic*]. His life story is a great story.[4]

Newspaper editors wanted to sell their product, and they recognized a "hot" story when they saw it. Ford's life had all the necessary elements ready to mold into the ever popular Horatio Alger myth of the rural boy turned millionaire. After these stories ran in the dailies, no longer was the Ford name recognized as solely a brand name. Ford products were now personified by Henry Ford—the Model T was Henry Ford incarnate, after all. Dixon Wector goes as far as to say that the Model T was "made in [Ford's] own image, a masterpiece of gaunt utility, pandering neither in beauty nor comfort that his Puritan soul distrusted."[5] By the time the newspapers were finished with the five-dollar day and Henry Ford, Ford's image was permanently established and would be presented to the public time and again over the decades to come.

That presentation, however, lay in the future. For the time being Henry Ford was such a stranger to the national scene that prior to the announcement of the five-dollar day the *New York Times Index* of 1913 did not place him on its *Who's Who* list, even though Ford had paid out over twelve million dollars that same year to twelve stockholders and bonuses to executives in the hundreds of thousands of dollars. Nor was Ford on the list even after ordering John R. Lee, head of Ford Motor Company employment, to take the unprecedented move of restructuring the wage system due to the fact that men, on the average, were quitting after only eighteen months on the job. After visiting several automotive manufacturers, Lee found that Ford Motor Company already paid the highest wages in the industry. He also found that Ford Motor Company provided the safest environment for its employees. However, Lee did find that workmen were leaving, in part, because company foremen carried too much power. The Ford foremen had the ability to give raises, to set a man's schedule, and to fire a man without reason. On hearing the report, Ford gave Lee permission to do whatever it would take to better labor relations.

Lee started by taking the power to grant pay increases out of the hands of foremen and by giving every worker a 13 percent pay raise, bringing the average salary of each man to $2.34 a day. At the same time, Lee took away the power of a foreman to dismiss a man. Instead, if a man was not performing to standards, a foreman could ask for the employee to be transferred out of his department, but he could not fire him.

These steps curtailed the number of men leaving, but they did not completely solve the unrest within the Ford workforce. When Ford and his son, Edsel, witnessed a fistfight between two men on the factory floor, it moved Ford to call a Board of Directors meeting for the purpose of discussing how to divide profits among stockholders, executives, customers, and labor.

Present at the Sunday, January 3, 1914, meeting were James Couzens, P. E. Martin, John R. Lee, Harold Willis, Norval Hawkins, and Charles Sorensen. Ford started by saying,

> Our workers are not sharing in our good fortune. There are thousands out there in the shop who are not living as they should. Their homes are crowded and unsanitary. Wives are going out to work because their husbands are unable to support the family. They fill up their homes with roomers and boarders in order to help swell their income. It's all wrong—all wrong. It's especially bad for their children. By underpaying men we are bringing on a generation of children undernourished and underdeveloped morally and physically.[6]

At the conclusion of his opening remarks, Ford walked to a blackboard; he wrote out figures under the headings "materials," "overhead," and "labor." They clearly supported the idea that as production increased, costs fell and profits grew. When Ford moved the margin of profit over to the labor column he figured what it would cost the company to pay each man $3.00 a day; then $3.50, $3.75, $4.25, $4.50, and then $4.75. Willis supported the measure; Martin protested. Couzens, who had up to this point kept his feelings hidden, spoke up, saying, "Well, so it's up to $4.75. I dare you to make it $5.00!"[7]

The minutes from the January 5, 1914, meeting of the Board of Directors, showing only Henry Ford, H. H. Rackham, and James Couzens present, demonstrate that Ford did just that after "the plan was gone over at considerable length."[8] The minutes read as follows.

> In addition to wages, sums to make the minimum income of all men over twenty-two years of age $5.00 for eight hours work, and that other increases are to be made to men getting above the minimum, intermediate and maximum wages.
>
> After considerable discussion it was moved by Director Rackham, and supported by Director Couzens, that such a plan be put into force as of January 12, 1914, which plan it was distinctly understood would approximate an additional expenditure for the same volume of business of Ten Million ($10,000,000.00) Dollars, for the year 1914. Carried unanimously.
>
> There being no further business, the meeting then adjourned.[9]

By midmorning of the same day, Ford and Couzens called a local news conference. The *Detroit Free Press, Detroit News,* and *Detroit Journal* were invited. Couzens read from a prepared statement.

> The Ford Motor Company, the greatest and most successful automobile manufacturing company in the world, will, on January 12, inaugurate the greatest revolution in the matter of rewards for its workers ever known to the industrial world.
>
> At one stroke it will reduce the hours of labor from nine to eight, and add to every man's pay a share of the profits of the house. The smallest amount to be received by a man 22 years old and upwards will be $5 per day. The minimum wage is now $2.34 per day at nine hours. . . .
>
> The factory is now working 2 shifts of nine hours each. This will

In the article accompanying this cartoon, the unidentified writer commented, "To make a sensation, be one. Then other people will attend to it—people in general, people going by in the streets—anybody and everybody will do your advertising for you and do it for nothing. Henry L. Ford has never needed to hunt up some way of making a stir or sensation. The Ford Car at its price has been a stir or sensation of itself." Note the middle initial "L." in Ford's name. He was so new to the popular scene that reporters and writers did not know that Henry Ford did not have a middle name. Variations of his middle initial can be found in a number of publications during this time. Note also how Henry Ford is dressed and his lean appearance. (From *New York Times Magazine,* New York, March 14, 1914.)

be changed to 3 shifts of eight hours each. The number employed is now about 15,000 and this will be increased by 4,000 or 5,000.

This will apply to every man of 22 years of age or upward without regard to the nature of his employment. In order that the young man from 18 to 22 years of age may be entitled to a share in the profits he must show himself sober, saving, steady, industrious and must satisfy the superintendent and staff that his money will not be wasted on riotous living.

It is estimated that over $10,000,000 will be thus distributed over and above the regular wages of mean.[10]

Of his five-dollar day, Henry Ford said, "There are thousands of men out there in the shop who are not living as they should. . . . Give them a decent income and they will live decently—will be glad to do so. What they need is the opportunity to do better, and someone to take a little personal interest in them—someone who will show that he has faith in them" (quoted in Samuel S. Marquis, *Henry Ford: An Interpretation*). Henry Ford was becoming this "someone," the Emersonian hero who would "make us do what we can do." This cartoon, published a few days after Ford's announcement, shows a profile of Henry Ford, a profile that looks more like Abraham Lincoln than Henry Ford. The artist's choice to depict Henry Ford in this way raises an interesting question: Did the artist know what Henry Ford looked like, or was the artist being introduced to Henry Ford for the first time just like everybody else? (From *Fort Wayne Sentinel*, Fort Wayne, Indiana, January 9, 1914.)

The local papers ran the story that evening under banner headlines. By the next morning reporters poured into Detroit from all over the world. By January 6, the story broke nationally and internationally. Reactions were mixed: the *Cleveland Plain Dealer* called the announcement a "shot like a blinding rocket through the dark clouds of the present industrial depression"; the *New York Herald* referred to the announcement as "an epoch in the world's industrial history"; the *Toledo Blade* termed it a "lordly gift" to Ford workers; the *New York Evening Post* credited the company with "a magnificent act of generosity"; the *New York World* called Ford "an inspired millionaire"; the *Algonac (Michigan) Courier* ran the headline "God Bless Henry Ford of the Ford Motor Company" over a story that referred to the manufacturer as "one of God's noblemen"; the *Ottawa (Illinois) Journal* ran the headline "Biggest Melon Cutting Begun, Ford Auto Company Gives $10,000,000 to Employees, Wages Doubled for 1914."[11]

Sermons inspired by the announcement lauded Ford's generosity: Dr. J. Percival Huget from the First Congregational Church said, "It is a most dramatic event and has touched the imagination of America and the world. And it is one chapter of a most interesting and dramatic life. The story of Henry Ford is one of the most interesting stories in all our American life."[12] At the Church of Our Father, Reverend Willis A. Moore declared the gift a new era in the relations between capital and labor. Reverend Luther E. Lovejoy at the Fourteenth Avenue Methodist Church stated that "we can see in this event a particular answer to the world's cry for social justice, the call of the toiling millions for a living wage and the longing of those who yearn for leisure, for self-improvement." "This is a big advance toward the day when the workingmen and the employer shall cease to be sworn enemies and will be friends and brothers," declared Rabbi Leo Franklin at the Temple Beth-El. Going further, Rabbi Franklin added, "If the workingman is to get the maximum wage, he must in return give the best of which he is capable."[13]

Ford employees gave interviews. Woljeck Manijklisjiski said of the move, "My boy don't sell no more papers. My girl don't work in the house of another and see her mother but once in the week no more. Again we are a family."

This new Ford model was inspired after a number of headlines and articles used the word *melon* to describe the sharing of Ford profits. Ford employees wore their employee badges proudly when going out on the town or to church. Some could finally afford to buy the very car they had been manufacturing for a number of years. So huge was the Ford employee wage that doctors, bankers, and lawyers left their jobs for an opportunity to join their ranks. Cartoonists concentrated on the subject of the five-dollar day as they and the rest of the country continued to learn more about Henry Ford from biographies published in a variety of sources. (From *Grand Rapids Press*, Grand Rapids, Michigan, January 7, 1914.)

Joshua (Tub) McMannigal, a Ford subforeman in the machinery room, added, "The big worry that leads a lot of fellows to the suicide route, and a lot more to the booze route, is just a lot of little worries added together mostly, and that's exactly what the big boost in pay is going to do away with in the Ford plant." The unidentified reporter who interviewed the two men added that

these two tried to express in concrete form the great wave that has swept over the factory, the wave that is the singing of happy men, the wave that has brought a lightness in step, a smile that glows through mask of oil and dirt, a lifting of tired shoulders, a gleam of manhood to eyes that were weary, a dawn of a new day to visions that had long known only the gloom of a dull existence.[14]

Some reporters even found a story in comparing wages and working conditions at the International Harvester Company to those at the Ford Motor Company.[15] An "investigative reporter" for the *Detroit Times* wrote

> Most of the [International Harvester employees] need charity. Some of them—those in dire distress—get it. The houses—most of them—are unsanitary, unhealthy, veritable disease-breeding spots. . . . If a man is killed in the works, his family is given three years wages. If a workman has an eye gouged out, the company hands him over three-fourths of his year's wage.[16]

The favorable response to Ford's announcement was met with an equal amount of negative reaction. In a preview to an editorial that would run on January 7, the *New York Times* said, "The theory of the management at Ford Motor Company is distinctly Utopian and runs dead against all experience. The movement for the bettering of society need not be universal in their opinion that one concern can make a start and create an example for other employers, that is our chief object."[17] The Employers Association of Detroit said that Ford was trying to undermine the structure of the capitalist system.[18] The *Rochester (New York) Union* reported that the general opinion of automotive manufacturers was that Ford's move was "too radical a step to take without consulting other automobile manufacturers. It would be utterly impossible for other manufacturers to take up the plan."[19] The *Toronto Globe* reported that

> [Ford] thinks he can confer favor by "giving" work, and feels that each extra effort by the worker, each extra five minutes, and each extra service is but a partial return for the favor he confers. This feeling prompts gradual and almost imperceptible encroachments which lead inevitably to an organized trades union defense, with demands for inelastic, inconvenient, and sometimes impossible limitations.[20]

THE TIED MAN AND THE FREE!

Critics of Ford's investment in his employees claimed that he was giving away money people should earn. Some detractors said that Ford was out to fill his factories with a talent pool unmatched by others. This cartoon compared the hope radiated by a Ford employee to the International Harvester employee sitting chained to poverty. A survey conducted by the Curtis Publishing Company in 1937 ranked Ford Motor Company number one in the treatment of its employees. This survey testified to the reputation established by the company in the second and third decades of the twentieth century. At first glance, the Ford employee in this cartoon reminds one of Henry Ford himself. This is understandable when one considers that the cartoon ran a few months after the five-dollar-a-day announcement. This would have provided the cartoonist with time to study Ford's appearance, and, most important, it would have given readers time to do the same. (From *Detroit Times*, Detroit, Michigan, April 17, 1914.)

Under the heading "Sensationalism in Profit Sharing," the *London Spectator* described Ford as "an enthusiast whose good intentions none question, but who is guided by his heart rather than his head. . . . It is not a stimulus to better work: it is a charitable gift to persons who happen to be in Mr. Ford's employment and as such it possesses all the disadvantages of benevolent schemes that have not been carefully thought out."[21]

However, no newspaper attacked Ford's announcement more vehemently than the *Wall Street Journal*, when it ran its story on January 7, which read as follows.

> Had Henry Ford set aside a fund that would insure the continuance of present wages paid to faithful employees, or a pension of half their wages after years of faithful service, it would have been scientific, and according to the highest ethics and the true laws of giving.
>
> But to inject ten millions into a company's factory, and to double the minimum wage, without regard to length of service, is to apply Biblical or spiritual principles into a field where they do not belong. . . .
>
> Such unscientific rewards may get advertising and get riddance to Henry Ford of his burdensome millions, but they are unscientific and not true charity in its broadest sense. . . .
>
> If the newspapers of the day are correctly reporting the latest invention and advertisement of Henry Ford he has in his social endeavor committed economic blunders, if not crimes. They may return to plague him and the industry he represents, as well as organized society.[22]

In the days following this bold decision, the world was introduced to Henry Ford—the boy, the man, and the industrial giant. "The conservative *New York Times* ran thirty-five stories on Ford within ninety days of the profit-sharing announcements, and no fewer than fourteen magazines carried biographies of the manufacturer during 1914."[23] In an advertisement for its Sunday edition following the announcement, the *New York Times* described Ford as "a farm boy who had a bent for mechanics; now a tall, slender man of fifty, throbbing with energy, radiating hope, a fighter of monopoly, a lover of birds and flowers and of the simple life. . . . His life story is a great story."

In its biographical article, entitled "Henry Ford, Who Made 26,000 Employees Happy," the *New York Sun* wrote that

> forty years ago he was doing chores on his father's farm at Dearborn, Michigan, six miles from Detroit. Twenty-five years ago he was drawing a mechanic's wages. Today he is giving away millions of dollars. . . . In the first place, be it said, Henry Ford seems to have been

SOME BUMP !

Ford, James Couzens, and the Model T were the gods that would bring judgment against the "kings" of industry and business. Belief in the divine rights of kings is the belief that monarchs get their right to rule directly from God, rather than from the consent or wish of their subjects. According to this concept, it is up to God to punish a wicked king. Notice here how the little Model T has grown in stature as it unites with its inventor and his right hand man while fighting for the common good and rolling past those that ridicule them and believe in the old system of leadership and economics. (From *Detroit Times,* Detroit, Michigan, January 7, 1914.)

endowed with mechanical genius as distinctly as great painters, great musicians, great poets, are specially endowed for their respective careers in the world. . . . While a farmer's boy out in Michigan he attended a country school until the time came for him to quit book study and go regularly to work in the field and orchards. He played games now and then with other lads, but usually when he had any spare time it was spent in constructing machines like a marvelous water wheel, for the edification and wonderment of all his companions.[24]

As a boy Ford repaired clocks and pocket watches for friends and neighbors. His mother said that clocks shuddered when Henry walked by. He did not care for farmwork, and he left home at age sixteen for the big city of Detroit. The young Henry Ford at his workbench became one of the many images people had of Ford as biographies about him were published in newspapers after his five-dollar-a-day announcement. Fourteen years later, during the height of the Model A's debut, the *New York Daily Mirror* reintroduced the legendary figure of Henry Ford to a whole new generation. The paper's editors did this by publishing a cartoon of Henry sitting at a workbench repairing a watch. In an article for *Time Magazine* on the top one hundred titans of business and industry, published in 1998, Lee Iacocca reminded us all once again that Henry left home at sixteen and walked into Detroit to start his career—if only we could all be as brave, just look at what we could do! Fittingly enough, in the same issue of *Time Magazine,* Ford's Model T is ranked number one in an article titled "Cars That Mattered." (From *New York Daily Mirror,* New York, ca. 1927.)

These early descriptions of Ford in the press, from his background, to his appearance, to his genius, became the traits and themes cartoonists favored in their renderings of Ford for the remainder of his life. Many of these traits and themes paralleled those found in cartoons about the Model T: Henry Ford was industrious, no nonsense, a self-made man, and a part of rural America. Ford took advantage of this newfound fame to point out that this was not the first time that Ford Motor Company had made a move for the benefit of its employees. "We have been paying wages 35 percent higher than other automobile manufacturers ever since our business was put on a paying basis," Ford stated, "and ever since I started in I have been trying to pay over a share of the profits to every person working for the success of the company."[25]

Meanwhile, Couzens used the press to lay a platform of caution by saying that Ford and the Board of Directors "did not know just how it will work out, or what our attitude regarding it will be at the end of the present year of the initial experiment. Experience will determine whether we will increase the minimum wage, or lower it; all will depend upon our careful observation of the working out of the scheme during the coming twelve months."[26]

An unidentified *New York Sun* reporter captured the moment best when writing "if Mr. Ford wins out with even approximate success not only will he be known as a wholesale Santa Claus but he will go down in history as the first human being who has ever been able to defy the law of supply and demand."[27]

In just two days following the announcement thousands of men gathered at the Highland Park employment office. On January 7, the *Detroit Free Press* ran the headline "Gold Rush on at Ford Plant; Mob for Jobs." The subheading read "Nucleus of 10,000 Crowd Forms at 2 o'clock in Morning."[28] The *Detroit Free Press* described the men as storming the employment office at the Ford plant. These were men of all nationalities and races; "unemployed men and men whose jobs suddenly had grown distasteful; rough-handed, white-collared men, eager to trade bookkeepers' stools for manual labor in the gasoline Golconda where even the sweepers get $5 a day."[29]

DOWN THAT CHIMNEY?

The image of Ford as Santa Claus emerged when a reporter dubbed him a "wholesale Santa Claus" in reference to his five-dollar-a-day gift. It was an image of Ford that reappeared in cartoons for the remainder of Ford's life. In this cartoon, published in 1915, the automaker endeavors to bring peace to Europe during his infamous peace ship voyage to Europe. (From *Brooklyn Eagle*, Brooklyn, New York, December 13, 1915.)

On Thursday, January 8, Ford plant inspectors took to walking through the crowd picking out men and piloting "them through the doors, presumably for hire. The number selected in this manner, however, was small." Men were selected for their known skill and excellence of character at "out of the way places."[30] By Friday, January 9, the *Detroit Free Press* reported that

In the ranks of the faithful was a different spirit, for departed were the jokes and banter, the good-humored contests for advantageous places in the lines, and the careless raillery which had made dragging hours seem shorter.

Silent and serious the men stood. It had become a serious business, this landing one of those $5-a-day-or-better jobs. . . .[31]

Exactly a week later, on January 12, the crowd had grown to over twelve thousand. Tempers were short, and tension was high— a riot broke out. In its last edition for January 12, 1914, the *Detroit Journal* described the episode as follows.

Monday morning the scene appeared to be about as normal as any day last week until close to 8 o'clock. Then the Ford employees began to appear in large numbers to go to work. They found the street so congested that entrance was difficult. The police were holding back the job-seekers so as to leave a lane for the employees, but the latter arrived so rapidly that they soon filled all the space left and soon the job-holders and job-seekers were thoroughly mingled.

The Ford employes [*sic*] wore little badges, but as the dense crowd jammed toward the single door that was open the police found it difficult to see just who got in. Soon there was such a congestion that no one could move. The police shouted orders until they were hoarse, but without effect. Then they threatened the crowd with the fire hose, but the crowd would not listen. The job-holders kept pressing forward and the job-seekers clung to them. Many could not do otherwise because of the enormous pressure on them from behind.

Then the police turned on the water, and employees, job-seekers and police officers themselves were drenched in short order. Scrambling backward the mob overturned lunch, cigar and other stands across Manchester avenue. Some men, drenched and angry, picked up bricks, stones and bottles and hurled them at the hose users. Many of these missiles went through the factory window.[32]

Men were arrested and taken away to jail, while others stopped into nearby bars to warm up and to buy a shot of whiskey. Others boarded the streetcar that ran down Woodward Avenue and headed into Detroit, where they hoped to find a place to sleep through the night. Highland Park police chief Seymor "defended his method of dealing with the near-riot by blaming Ford manage-

COMEDY OR TRAGEDY?—By. DeBeck.

A day after the five-dollar-a-day announcement, men gladly waited in front of the Highland Park plant employment office. Some people joked and played cards. Some people played games that allowed them to move up in line one person at a time. In a place where even the floor sweeper was paid five dollars a day and dressed in top hat and tails, the wait was worth the trouble. But by January 8 men were becoming restless, and by January 12 a riot broke out. Ford and his company were criticized for not being prepared to handle the massive crowd. After the riot, everyone was left with the question, was Ford's generosity a comedy or a tragedy? (From *Pittsburgh Gazette*, Pittsburgh, Pennsylvania, January 8, 1914.)

THE GERMS OF SOCIALISM.

This cartoon draws on memories Americans had of the great strikes in Russia that led to communist takeover in 1905. Note the peasant costume of the farmer and the demand for a share of profits from the boy. The cartoon was humorous but echoed the sentiment of those in big business, who felt Ford had given away what employees should earn through years of hard work. (From *Cincinnati Times-Star,* Cincinnati, Ohio, January 9, 1914.)

ment for making such a dramatic disclosure without devising some way to control the inevitable stampede."[33]

The riot stole headlines. Ford was concerned that his five-dollar day had created more problems than good; unemployed men loitered around the factory; men refused jobs elsewhere because they did not pay five dollars a day. Even after the riot, people kept

The Ford Sociological Department made sure that employees saved their money or spent it on just causes. Field representatives visited employees' homes to make sure that excess was not being practiced. If employees were found guilty, their five-dollar pay increase was taken away, and inappropriate behavior could result in termination. "Big Brother" Henry Ford was definitely watching. This cartoon joked that Ford employees studied guides and "how to" books—in this case, a how to dress book—to avoid jeopardizing their five-dollar-a-day jobs. (From *New York Globe*, New York, 1914.)

lining up at the factory. Letters poured in by the thousands asking Ford for jobs. Meanwhile, the newly hired and veteran Ford employees realized that the five-dollar day came with certain restrictions, the most troublesome being visits to their homes by men belonging to the Ford Sociological Department, a department started in 1913 for the purpose of teaching employees about a number of social behaviors that included how to clean a house, how to bathe, how to brush teeth, how to sanitize the kitchen sink, and so on. Most important, the department existed to make sure

Henry Ford rides in a Model T while he challenges Mars to "cut out" the rough-housing. This cartoon is from the peace ship period of Ford's life. The cartoon makes reference to Ford jokes, which were popular at the time. In years past, jokes were aimed at the Model T; now they were directed at Henry Ford. The period of the peace ship also established Henry Ford and the Model T as one and the same, at least in cartoons. (From *Sioux City Tribune,* Sioux City, Iowa, December 1, 1915.)

that men were not throwing their money away on smoking, gambling, drinking, or prostitution.

Ford soon earned the nickname the "mad socialist" because of this tactic. In addition, his name became a verb—*to Fordize* meant to do things the Henry Ford way—aggressively and without reservation; the Ford name also became a noun—*Fordism*—which referred to Ford's belief that profits should go to the consumer and employee.

By the end of the year, Ford's five-dollar day had provided Ford Motor Company with so much free press that the *Everett (Washington) Tribune* estimated the figure of free publicity at

$5,000,000; the *New York Times* at $10,000,000; and the *Syracuse Journal* at $20,000,000. Of course, the final success or failure of the five-dollar day lay on the results of the bottom line; that was really all that mattered. When car sales for 1914 were tallied and compared to those of 1913, they showed an increase of 80,003. When dollar amounts were compared, they showed an increase of $30,380,432.43 from 1913 to 1914.[34]

By these measures it appeared that Ford's five-dollar-a-day experiment had succeeded, and as the year came to an end, Ford began to shed his "shy" ways; he had an opinion on everything from smoking to the gold standard. He also had an opinion on war, an opinion that was soon to put the "wholesale Santa Claus" on the front pages of national and international newspapers yet again. The timing could not have been better for both Henry Ford and his Model T, because they were now two icons that were recognized by Americans, and the world, as one and the same. With the launching of the "peace ship" this dual identity would become a standard feature of the editorial and political cartoons on Henry Ford. Always together during the voyage of the peace ship, Ford and the Model T can be seen fighting gods of war or chugging along past those whose advice to stop their ridiculous efforts they ignored.

CHAPTER 3

Man Overboard: The Lampooning
of Ford's Peace Ship

IF THE FIVE-DOLLAR-A-DAY ANNOUNCEMENT planted the seed
of the image of Henry Ford as an ingenious country boy made
good who could do no wrong, his plan to end World War I by
means of a peace ship served to remind us that Henry Ford was
only a man, a human being who made mistakes. Few Americans
today know that once upon a time Henry Ford, one of the wealth-
iest men in America, chartered a ship to Europe hoping to insti-
gate peace talks that would bring World War I to an end. Like
Ford's announcement of his five-dollar day, his plan for peace
received international coverage in newspapers. Ford's initiative, as
reported by editorial cartoonists, lasted from the beginning of the
voyage until several months after the event ended. However,
unlike the cartoons that had come before, cartoons on this topic
featured Henry Ford and, on occasion, Henry Ford and his Model
T. As far as cartoonists were concerned Ford's announcement of
his peace ship could not have come at a better time, because they
now knew Henry Ford from the biographies published about him
and, most important, the world knew Henry Ford.

From these biographies and the five-dollar-a-day event, cartoonists and the public took with them the image of Henry Ford as
a lean, firm standing, and well-dressed farm boy. Furthermore, he
was a self-made man, someone who thought of others before himself. He also did things his way, or he did not do them at all. These
physical attributes, as well as his personal and professional philoso-
phies, were by now well established in people's minds and in the
popular culture of the time. When combined with the reputation
held by the Model T, both good and bad, Henry Ford provided a
wealth of material for editorial cartoonists. These cartoons cut
deep; some supported his convictions, while others damned him

for his efforts. Those people that did not care for Ford's Model T, or for Ford the man, certainly took notice of him at this time, especially since a large number of these citizens had boys fighting in Europe.

The events that led to Ford's peace ship started in June 1915 when Ford held a press conference to unveil his working gasoline tractor, which Ford promoted as a tool to make life easier for farmers. At this conference Ford commented on the war in Europe. Like many Americans from the Midwest, Ford opposed war.

Directly after this press conference, a reporter for the *Detroit Free Press,* Theodore Delavigne, was sent by the editor to delve more deeply into the auto manufacturer's thoughts on the war in Europe. Ford granted an interview, and his views, which remained unchanged, were published. Delavigne, who eventually became Ford's personal "peace secretary," penned an article in November 1915 that proclaimed in its headline, "Henry Ford to Push World-Wide Campaign for Universal Peace: Will Devote Life and Fortune to Combat Spirit of Militarism Now Rampant."[1]

A later article detailed further how Ford envisioned his new tractor as an instrument of peace. He felt that businesspeople could and should make money from peace and the promotion of peace. Ford's offer to finance projects that promoted peace in Europe attracted all sorts of people, from eccentrics to con artists. Fortunately, Henry Ford was protected from the crowds of suppliants by his private secretary, Ernest G. Liebold. However, one woman managed to gain an audience with Ford while Liebold was out of town. Her name was Rosika Schwimmer, and she was a Hungarian native, an author, a lecturer, and a well-known pacifist. By this time, Madame Schwimmer's reputation as an overly aggressive campaigner for peace and the women's rights movement had alienated her from many of the mainstream pacifists in America. She had even managed to meet with President Wilson to discuss her ideas but to no avail. Madame Schwimmer claimed to have documentation from the European heads of state that proved that they wanted peace if only a way could be found to iron out their differences. She felt sure that all that was needed was an independent negotiating body made up of American pacifists to bring this

HENRY'S DREAM

With news of the five-dollar day behind him, Ford now made international headlines by announcing that he would stop World War I by Christmas of the year
1915. Ford would put a stop to deeply entrenched "Militarism" by using the
strength of his Model T and a rope made of "Ford Millions" to get the job done.
Ford's peace ship venture would be covered from start to finish by cartoonists.
These cartoons would be the first to feature Ford the man in a prominent role.
(From *New York Telegram*, New York, November 27, 1915.)

to reality. Madame Schwimmer found that Henry Ford's generous offer of monetary assistance in the *Detroit Free Press* matched perfectly with her need for funds to create this impartial delegation for peace. At the time of her meeting with Ford she was on a lecture tour for the American Peace Society. Their first meeting was at the Ford factory on November 17. Ford liked what Schwimmer said and invited her to his house the next day. She arrived with fellow pacifist Louis P. Lochner and wasted no time in convincing Ford of the value of his assistance.

Ford, excited about Madame Schwimmer's call to action, left the woman with his wife, Clara, to see what she thought about Schwimmer's ideas. By afternoon, Madame Schwimmer had convinced Clara to head a telegraph campaign by American mothers against the war at a cost of ten thousand dollars. This acceptance from the normally frugal Clara Ford must have sealed Ford's belief in Schwimmer, since he often sought Clara's advice on benevolent undertakings and she was no easy target. In making her contribution Clara made a statement to the press that read as follows.

> Happy in my own motherhood and sympathizing with the bitter sorrow of the mothers bereaved by war, I want to foster a demonstration enabling American women to go on record as favoring a conference of neutral nations working toward a just settlement of the great European tragedy.[2]

Ford made hasty arrangements to travel first to New York and then to Washington to see President Wilson the following day on behalf of the movement. Ford felt New York would be the ideal place to drum up publicity. He also had full confidence that he could secure support from Wilson on whatever project the American Peace Society proposed.

Prior to his meeting with President Wilson, Ford met with a number of peace delegates at a luncheon at the McAlpin Hotel on November 19 to discuss strategy. It was here that the idea of a peace ship was first proposed by Louis P. Lochner, Madame Schwimmer's companion at the Fords' house. He offered the suggestion more in jest than as a real possibility. Many of the delegates to the meeting, especially noted activist Jane Addams, objected

Trying To Paint A Rainbow Of Peace.

He thinks that he'll "splash at a ten-league canvas with brushes of comet's hair."

In cartoons that came after Ford's announcement of a peace ship, Ford is seen as an idealistic man. In this cartoon Ford, dressed in his trademark suit, does not seem to understand the scope of the challenge ahead of him. This, however, does not stop him from painting the world as he sees it. On military preparedness, Ford stated, "I don't believe in preparedness. It's like a man carrying a gun. Men and nations who carry guns get into trouble. If I had my way, I'd throw every ounce of gunpowder into the sea and strip soldiers of their insignias" ("I Don't Believe in Preparedness," *Detroit Times*, 19 April 1916). From *Baltimore Sun*, Baltimore, Maryland, November 26, 1915.)

strongly to the very extravagant nature of this idea, but the boldness of the idea caught Mr. Ford's attention and propelled him to action. He took charge of the endeavor over the objections of many present.

Ford immediately began searching for a vessel. That same day he chartered the SS *Oscar II*, a Scandinavian-American liner due to leave New York in eleven days. Ford had a meeting scheduled with President Wilson the very next day at which he planned to invite the president aboard the ship. Delegates from the luncheon hoped that Mr. Ford would delay making plans for a peace ship until they could better organize the project and secure a commitment from the U.S. government, which would add credibility to the undertaking. Selected members pushed for the idea to be dropped altogether in favor of a more traditional resolve. Ford saw no need for this hesitation and continued with his plans.

Nuts

Once Ford chartered the Scandinavian-American ocean liner *Oscar II* to carry his peace delegates to Europe, cartoonists had a new component to add to the growing lore. In this case, the *Oscar II* became the bowl containing a variety of nuts, reflecting many observers' view of the passengers on the *Oscar II*. In this cartoon, we also see the character Mars, the Roman god of war, making one of his first appearances in a cartoon dealing with Ford's plan for peace. Mars representing war in cartoons, however, was nothing new to readers. (From *St. Louis Star,* St. Louis, Missouri, December 1, 1915.)

Woodrow Wilson did not want to meet with Henry Ford, but Wilson knew that turning Ford down would make it look as though the president did not support the peace movement. Ford naively tried to put the president at ease by being as casual as possible. Ford draped one leg over the arm of his chair and proceeded to tell a Model T joke he had made up about how a man wanted to be buried in his Model T because it had gotten him out of every hole he had ever been in. Wilson recited a limerick in return, and Ford felt the meeting was going to be a success until the president with a great deal of diplomatic double-talk turned him down flat.[3] He would not support the venture in any way. Ford was visibly put off and declared that he would go ahead and announce his plans for a peace ship at 10 A.M. the next day. Ford's final words to Wilson were, "If you don't act, I will."[4]

On November 24, 1915, true to his word, Ford called a disorganized press conference to announce his plans for a peace ship. Ford, surprised by the large turnout, was not very articulate. He started out by making the simple statement that he had a ship.

> "What ship, Mr. Ford?" a reporter asked.
> "Why the *Oscar II*."
> "Well, what are you going to do with her?"
> "We're going to stop the war."
> "Going to stop the war?"
> "Yes, we're going to get the boys out of the trenches by Christmas."
> "But how are you going to do it?"
> "Oh, you'll see."
> "Where are you going?"
> "I don't know."
> "But what makes you think you can put it over?"
> "Oh, we have had assurances."[5]

Ford's indecisiveness and lack of concrete plans left the press skeptical. The *Detroit Free Press* wrote that "Repeated questions disclosed not the slightest evidence that Mr. Ford has a definite plan as to what he is going to do when he gets to Europe."[6] The *New York Tribune*'s headline the next morning read "GREAT WAR TO END CHRISTMAS DAY: FORD TO STOP IT."[7] Ford's performance cre-

Rosika Schwimmer stands on the back of a peace delegate as she strains to listen at a White House window. She listens, no doubt, to Ford's conversation with President Wilson. Schwimmer had met with President Wilson prior to going to Ford but to no avail. A *Detroit Journal* reporter described Schwimmer as stocky, with an "owl-like" face and bulldog jaw. Her front teeth were separated, and her "clothing, which he judged typical suffragist: plumed hat, double-breasted suit, cotton stockings, and button boots," left her with the appearance of being much older than her thirty-eight years. (From *New York Herald*, New York, November 1915.)

ated an undercurrent of ridicule that found its way onto the editorial pages of most major newspapers. Ford's off-the-cuff remark that "We're going to get the boys out of the trenches by Christmas" added fuel to the fire. The *New York World* said that stopping the war was "something that money will not do." The *Baltimore Evening Sun* added, "It ought to be apparent to all intelligent people that Woodrow Wilson is just waiting anxiously for an opening that promises success to make a move to end the war." The *Louisville Courier Journal* held nothing back when it reported that "it is worse than ineffable folly for pestiferous busybodies in this country like Henry Ford and Jane Addams to nag the president to make an ass of himself by mediating in behalf of a peace which is impossible."[8]

What followed in the weeks before the *Oscar II* left was a flood of caricatures of Henry Ford puttering along in an undersized Model T headed toward the war in Europe. There were as many variations on this image as there were papers in the United States. At first the drawings were good humored in nature and followed the well-promoted idea that the Model T could conquer problems twice its size.

Two days before the journey of the *Oscar II,* one of the most poignant political cartoons concerning Ford up to that time commented on Ford's excursion. Published in the *Evening World* in New York, the cartoon pictured Ford as an oversized clown entering a circus tent labeled "European War" with a deflated balloon labeled "peace" dragging on the ground. The usual good humor that most often accompanied criticism of Ford is nowhere to be found. Instead, he is a clown going into a darkened circus tent with nothing but his idealistic views as ammunition.

When the day of departure arrived—December 4, 1915—quite an odd assortment of people awaited the big event at the pier in Hoboken, New Jersey. On board with Ford were 83 peace delegates made up of members of the American Peace Society and other dignitaries invited by Henry Ford. Along with this main group came 50 people employed as support staff, 54 reporters, 3 photographers, and 18 college students also invited by Ford. This flamboyant, hopelessly idealistic expedition departed without government backing and with little organization.[9]

Cranking Up.

The day after Ford's announcement that he, along with his entourage, was "going to get the boys out of the trenches by Christmas," a drawing appeared showing Ford with a Model T crank to his head. The artist apparently had no idea what Ford's face looked like, because the cartoon image bears no resemblance to Henry Ford. (From *New York Herald*, New York, November 25, 1915.)

William Jennings Bryan attended the launching just so he could be seen supporting the latest peace efforts. Fifteen minutes before the ship was to sail an anonymous prankster sent a messenger to the dock in a taxicab. The messenger boy carried a "large covered cage which was said to contain a live dove. When the cage was uncovered, however, it was found that the occupant was a large gray squirrel."[10] Needless to say, the squirrel became the mascot

"WELL, DAVID DID T."—By Brinkerhoff.

"David Ford" lifts rocks marked with a dollar sign, as "Goliath Mars" waits to do battle behind him, no doubt with a smile on his face. A number of cartoons in Ford's career pictured the diminutive and idealistic Ford against a much larger and stronger opponent. (From *New York Mail,* New York, November 29, 1915.)

for the voyage, countering the image of the dove of peace. Cartoonists soon took advantage of the occasion, showing the squirrel in a variety of situations among the "nuts" on the ship.

Perhaps the biggest heartbreak for Ford was the fact that while his mentor Thomas A. Edison came to the pier to see him off, Edison pretended not to hear when Ford said he would give him a million dollars to come along. Even Clara and Edsel Ford abandoned

POOR OLD DOVE

Ford's method of a "quick peace" challenged the approach toward peace of President Wilson's ex–secretary of state, William Jennings Bryan, which was to settle disputes through international arbitration. Even though Bryan had managed to negotiate at least two dozen treaties promoting peace, his methods were too slow for Henry Ford. In the cartoon, Ford and Bryan enjoy a tug-of-war over the dove of peace as Jane Addams cries out for a peaceful settlement between the two men. (From *New York Telegram*, New York, November 30, 1915.)

If anyone could break through the snowdrift of war it was Henry Ford with his Model T. If Ford had a plan on how he was going to break through the drift he was not sharing it with anyone. As far as Ford was concerned peace would come as follows: "The moment we can get people not to acquiesce in war, to refuse to go to war, there will be no more war. Only the rulers will be left to fight. Such contests would be little prize fights between kings" (quoted in William C. Richards, *The Last Billionaire*). (From *Springfield News*, Springfield, Illinois, December 2, 1915.)

The Clown ❧ ❧ By J. H. Cassel

Ford steps into the big top of the European war dressed as a clown and dragging a deflated balloon labeled "peace." Cartoons such as this one reiterated the point that Ford had no idea what he was getting himself into, and they pointed out the humor found in the idea that one man sincerely felt he could stop a world war single-handedly. (From *New York Evening World*, New York, December 2, 1915.)

the cause after Clara watched the wasteful spending of Madame Schwimmer with disapproval. She suddenly found the woman who had captured her heart a few weeks earlier to be nothing more than a flamboyant spendthrift. Unable to sway Ford not to go, Clara was comforted when Ford agreed that the family spiritual adviser, Reverend Samuel S. Marquis, could accompany him on the trip.

PEACE (at Home) - - - - - - - *By J. H. Cassel*

Ford's peace ship departed from a Hoboken, New Jersey pier on December 4, 1915. In this cartoon, a relieved Uncle Sam sits on the pier after Ford and his various malcontents were aboard and on their way. (From *Peoria Star*, Peoria, Illinois, December 12, 1915.)

As the ship pulled out of port, the delegates on board had a semblance of a plan: they were to land in Norway at Oslo and then go by land through Sweden, Denmark, and Holland. Along the way they would give lectures and hold meetings designed to stir up a general outcry for peace. However, there was no real itinerary, as evidenced in the fact that not a single hall had been reserved for these meetings.

Aboard the ship, delegates wore buttons whose design was

The Latest Ford Story.

The god of war, Mars, enjoys a hearty laugh at Ford's expense. There is no doubt that the nation's readers did the same after reading about Ford's peace ship. How one man thought he could bring an end to war was a story that would be hard to top, but as Mars exclaimed, this was only the best Ford story yet. Surely Ford, if anyone, could top this story with no problem. (From *St. Louis Globe Democrat*, St. Louis, Missouri, November 29, 1915.)

based on a poster that was created for the voyage showing a fist coming out of the ocean stopping Mars, the god of war, dead in his tracks. The actual delegates of the peace conference, Rosika Schwimmer's crowd, were rarely seen. They stayed behind closed doors making plans and talking. Ford remained surprisingly accessible even as the ridicule of editorials and cartoons grew. He scheduled press conferences that lasted two hours a day and then roamed freely among the crowds for the rest of the day. It was

By Gum, This Is the Funniest Joke of the Hull Lot!

In 1915 people were familiar with joke books about the Model T. In this cartoon, Uncle Sam introduces readers to his collection of joke books about Henry Ford. He chuckles, however, at the fact that the "funniest joke of the hull lot" is not found in the joke books but in the nation's newspapers. (From *Des Moines Capital*, Des Moines, Iowa, December 3, 1915.)

while he was walking around the deck talking to delegates and passengers that a rogue wave washed over Ford, causing him to come down with a cold that quickly turned into the flu.

To keep the world informed as to the business aboard the *Oscar II*, Ford had a wireless transmitter installed before departure. Ford used the new technology endlessly to send messages to the world about his mission. He had the Sunday sermon of Dr. Aked sent out, costing him over one hundred thousand dollars. Ford scoffed at the criticism of this overuse of the wireless by pointing

One commentator drew the peace ship as an opportune way to get rid of all the crackpots and annoying activists running about the country voicing their opinions on the war in Europe. (From *Boston Post*, Boston, Massachusetts, December 27, 1915.)

out that he made fifty million dollars a minute. Ford used the wireless to send messages to heads of state throughout Europe, first asking the nations to quit blaming each other, then noting commonalties that could be the basis for peace talks. A heartfelt cry for a truce ended these telegrams, which were signed

> For the sake of humanity,
> Respectfully Yours,
> Henry Ford
> And 165 representatives of the people of the United States of America.

SHIPLOAD OF HAZELS AND HICKORYS.

With the arrival of a squirrel in a cage fifteen minutes before the *Oscar II*'s departure for Europe, cartoonists now had a mascot to replace the oft used dove of peace. This prank was suggested by cartoons and stories that referred to Ford's shipmates as "nuts." The featured squirrels are quite an assortment of characters. Note the squirrel to the left driven to tears while exclaiming, "Barnum was right." Cartoons criticizing Ford often played off Barnum's famous comment, "There's a sucker born every minute." (From *New York Telegram,* New York, December 1915.)

WAITING

King Haakon, the chosen king of the Norwegian people after Norway's separation from Sweden in 1905, waits for Ford and the rest of his party. With nutcracker and squirrel cage in hand, the cartoon king hopes to make a good impression on Henry Ford by showing off his Model T toy at his feet. The popularity of the peace movement has even inspired the king in this cartoon to redesign the country's coat of arms, which now features nuts and the Model T. (From *New York Telegram,* New York, December 1915.)

Another phenomenon occurred aboard the *Oscar II* because of this wireless. Reporters constantly wired reports back to their papers, often jamming the airwaves and leading to rumors that Ford was censoring information, which was far from true. Ford actually encouraged as many stories as possible to be fed out over wireless in order to promote his cause.

In reality, there was not much to report anyway, that is, until four days later when President Wilson delivered his first "preparedness speech" to Congress asking for money, a better navy, and a citizen's army. At that same moment, on the *Oscar II*, S. S. McClure of *McClure's Magazine* was reading the president's speech to the inhabitants of the ship. McClure had obtained a copy through his editorial capacities. After reading the speech, McClure announced his support for the president. This announcement created a chaotic scene on board with people shouting their opinions at each other. While a statement from Ford tried to patch up differences, tranquility on the peace ship had left for good.

One newspaper man wired a story about a mutiny onboard that the Norwegians nearly took as a real distress call. The wireless allowed the discord on the ship to be broadcast around the world. Editorial cartoonists could not resist making this the subject of their satires.

It was about this same time that Ford's representatives engineered a mock fire alarm in order to go through the famous black bag of Madame Schwimmer, which she constantly reminded everyone she possessed. Inside the bag were no notes from heads of state supporting her cause or agreeing to meet with the American delegation as she had suggested all along. All that Ford's men found were the personal effects commonly found in most women's travel bags of the era. When Ford received the news, he lost all confidence in Schwimmer.

The peace ship finally docked in Oslo, Norway, on December 14, 1915. The flu that had overtaken Ford aboard the ship tightened its grip on the automaker. It was twenty-six below zero that first day, and Ford had to forge through several inches of snow to get to the hotel. His room there was dark and drafty, with a northern exposure making it oppressive and disheartening. Ford's spirits sank. The condition of Ford was kept a secret, leading a Dearborn, Michigan, paper to run the headline "Ford Dead!" He did not make a public appearance for five days. Finally, on December 22, Ford called a press conference where he spoke about his Fordson tractor and nothing else. The reporters were quite surprised, and one of them was heard saying, "He must be a very great man who permits himself to utter such foolishness."[11]

The New Ford Joke

By J. H. Cassel

A diminutive and dapper Henry Ford stands up to "War," asking him to stop the fighting. War sits in the trenches, which is a reference to Ford's claim that he would have the boys out of the trenches by Christmas. The title, "The New Ford Joke," reminds readers of the Model T jokes of the past but suggests that Ford-related jokes have found a whole new life with Ford's announcement of his peace ship. While many cartoonists continued to mock the peace ship, newspaper reporters aboard the ship actually started to respect Ford's efforts. According to David L. Lewis in *The Public Image of Henry Ford*, one reporter wrote that he "came to make fun of the whole thing, but my editor is going to have the surprise of his life. . . . I believe in Henry Ford and I'm going to say so." (From *New York World*, New York, November 27, 1915.)

BY WIRELESS FROM THE PEACE-SHIP.

In Wilson's first preparedness message to Congress, on December 7, he said that "if our citizens are ever to fight upon a sudden summons, they must know how modern fighting is done." Wilson also went on record in support of taxes on gasoline and automobiles. Wilson's message split the peace delegates. Some supported the president's message of preparedness, while others did not. This disagreement became the first news story to break from the *Oscar II*. By the next morning cartoons and articles ridiculed the bickering among those on board. Headlines read "War in Mid-Ocean," "Uproar on the Peace Ship," and "Mutiny on Board." (From *Minneapolis Daily News,* Minneapolis, Minnesota, December 11, 1915.)

THE ANGEL OF PEACE SEASICK

The angel of peace, an early mascot for the peace ship initiative, was featured in early cartoons riding side by side with Henry Ford in a Model T racing boldly to Europe. With the outbreak of a verbal war among peace delegates, the angel of peace was reduced to a seasick passenger, symbolizing the disenchantment of those on board the *Oscar II*. (From *Sacramento Bee*, Sacramento, California, December 8, 1915.)

The next day Ford, totally disillusioned with Madame Schwimmer and her peace accord, told the Reverend Marquis, "Guess I had better go home to Mother." On Christmas Eve, Ford's men were seen hauling a trunk out of the hotel at 4 A.M. Soon afterward, Ford and Reverend Marquis followed. Ford had informed Madame Schwimmer that he would be leaving that day, but no one anticipated this early departure. Members of Schwimmer's entourage that saw Ford leaving ran to get her, but they were too late. Ford and the Reverend Marquis had boarded an American-bound ship at Bergen, and there was no getting them back.

On the trip home, Ford and Reverend Marquis talked about what little had been accomplished and the consequences to come once back in the United States. Ford anticipated criticism, which

The peace ship finally docked in Oslo, Norway, on December 14, 1915. One artist captured the moment by recalling the comments of Charles Sorensen, a former Ford executive and close friend of Henry Ford, who stated that a stranger group of passengers on a ship had not been seen since Noah's ark. (From *New York Globe*, New York, 1915.)

indeed followed in newspaper accounts and editorial cartoons. In cartoons, Ford was seen as a man having learned his lesson. This gave the public a new image to ponder. It was very different from the powerful Henry Ford they had been introduced to a year before in portraits accompanying biographies. "I'll never make that mistake again!" Henry exclaims in one cartoon, and in another he says, "NEVER AGAIN!" To make the transformation complete one cartoon showed Ford as an overweight man dressed in a long coat and top hat. He wears gloves, and his checkered pants, hidden by the long coat, keep us from seeing just how much Ford has changed. Even Ford's face is not recognizable.

This negative press, however, was balanced by positive accounts that hailed Ford's heroic attempt at ending the war. The

In a letter to Madame Schwimmer, dated August 12, 1916, Clara Ford wrote that "The way Mr. Ford's name and money was used was shameful and you are the leader" (quoted in Barbara S. Kraft, *The Peace Ship: Henry Ford's Pacifist Adventure in the First World War*).

Of her expense account, Schwimmer had confided to Lochner with delight, "All I have to do is wave my wand and lo! it appears." Purchases charged to Ford included a "peace wardrobe" consisting of evening dresses and fur coats. (From *New York American*, New York, December 31, 1915.)

This cartoon aptly captures the fact that Ford returned to the United States after only nine days in Norway. It was as if Ford had walked to the European front, said nothing, done an about-face, and returned home. Once he left, however, his money financed peace initiatives that followed. (From *Washington Star*, Washington, DC, December 26, 1915.)

Saginaw (Michigan) Herald captured the sentiment contained in articles appearing around the country best when it wrote that Ford

> had sailed away a short time before, one of the most ridiculed men of his generation; he sailed back into an atmosphere of sympathy. In the meantime, his expedition had appealed to the imagination of his countrymen. The very hopelessness of the task he had attempted commanded a sort of respect. "God's Fool," the *Springfield Republican* calls him, striking in those two words perhaps the keynote of the comment of the majority of the journals of this country.[12]

T. E. POWERS, INTERNATIONAL NEWS SERVICE.

Ford returned from his peace ship venture to both jeers and cheers. A large percentage of cartoons ridiculed Ford for his failure to bring peace to Europe. In this cartoon, Ford's name is misspelled, the dove of peace walks beaten beside him, and the peace delegates left onboard fight and argue. On either side of "Hennery" the squirrels abandon ship. Ford's first name was often misspelled when cartoonists judged his behavior humorous. (From International News Service, 1915.)

With his Model T tucked safely under his arm and his party banners in tow, his
last "palm of peace" slipping out of his pocket, Ford returns home dragging a
can of Norwegian lobster. Traveling home, Ford told Reverend Marquis, "I do
not want the things money can buy. I want to live a life, to make the world a little
better for having lived in it" (quoted in Marquis, *Henry Ford: An Interpretation*).
(From *Washington Star*, Washington, DC, December 28, 1915.)

THE FIGHTING PACIFIST

Once the United States severed diplomatic ties with Germany, Ford threw his full support behind Allied forces. At the same time he promised not to benefit from his efforts. (From *London Illustrated News,* London, 1918.)

Even after this fiasco, Ford continued to finance projects for the American Peace Society until 1917, when Germany declared that they would resume submarine attacks on American ships.

Once diplomatic relations with Germany were severed, Ford, along with Woodrow Wilson and William Jennings Bryan, traded in his pacifist garments for a war uniform. German attacks were a direct assault on free enterprise and American business; Ford could not remain an advocate for peace any longer. However, even as Ford put his full resources behind the war, he promised not to profit from it. He vowed to return every penny that he made on war production, thus separating himself from the men he felt were only involved in supplying the armed forces for profit.

CHAPTER 4

Battle of a Different Sort: Henry Ford's Run for the U.S. Senate

AFTER HIS RETURN TO DETROIT from his failed mission to Europe, Ford remained a leading pacifist until the United States broke diplomatic relations with Germany on February 3, 1917. With ties to Germany severed, Ford immediately offered his factories to the U.S. government with the promise that he would operate the factories "without one cent profit."[1] He also promised to contribute his time to the war effort and "to work harder than ever before."[2]

In offering his factories to the American government, Ford claimed that he could use his mass production methods to build one thousand small submarines and three thousand motors in one day. He would accomplish this through Ford ingenuity. The submarine, for example, would be designed to carry one man. The man was to carry a pole in the submarine with him. Once the man had reached the side of his target, he would take the pole and attach a "pill-bomb" to the side of the ship's hull.

Neither Henry's offer nor his ideas were enough to get the American government to come calling. This did not deter Ford, who announced in August 1917 that he could produce 150,000 airplanes for the war effort in one year using his moving assembly line if given the chance. Ford started his move in this direction by asking his British business agent, Percival Perry, to send him captured plans of a German warplane. Perry advised Ford that he could not do that unless Ford was acting with permission granted by the U.S. government. On learning this, Ford turned his attention to convincing the government of his plan to build airplanes. When the government failed to take an interest in his objective, Ford abandoned the idea.[3]

The British, however, wasted no time in taking advantage of

STANDING BEHIND THE PRESIDENT

FORD FACTORIES

HENRY FORD
" ALL I HAVE IS AT
YOUR SERVICE"
UNCLE SAM

A grateful Uncle Sam accepts Ford's offer of his factories for use in wartime production. Known as a pacifist, Ford became a "fighting pacifist" after diplomatic relations were broken with Germany on February 3, 1917. The image of Ford, which shows him with sleeves rolled up and his vest unbuttoned, captured his commitment to the war effort. In offering his factories, Ford said that he was ready to contribute his energy to the war effort and "to work harder than ever before." Cartoons such as this one helped the public forget about Ford's peace ship fiasco and added to his growing popularity. (From *Buffalo News,* Buffalo, New York, March 22, 1917.)

Ford's offer of assistance. Although Ford's relationship with the British during the peace ship fiasco was strained, he knew that they needed tractors to cultivate land in order to produce enough food to feed their population of well over forty million. The British placed an order for seven thousand tractors. It was to be the first time that Ford had produced tractors using his method of mass production.

Et Tu Henry!

A skin and bones Ford leaves the White House after offering his factories to the war effort. William Jennings Bryan leaps off the ground in astonishment. Ford's Roman soldier's uniform is ill fitting, and his weapon is too small for the job ahead. This image once again is an attempt to show that Ford, as when he was involved in his peace efforts, does not fully understand what he is up against. He marches forward wearing the helmet that during the peace ship fiasco fit Mars, the god of war, so well. (From *Baltimore Sun*, Baltimore, Maryland, February 6, 1917.)

Meanwhile, on the home front, Ford developed a two-man tank and claimed that he could produce one thousand of them in one day. The army came calling, asking for a demonstration. The demonstration consisted of the small tanks, which the press (making use of a term frequently used to signify the Model T and other small, cheap automobiles) had dubbed "flivver tanks," crossing a field with trenches scattered about. When the tank went to cross one of the trenches, it became stuck, nose up. "What are you going

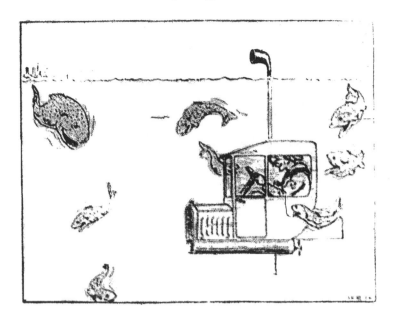

When Ford pledged to produce one thousand submarines a day, critics thought it impossible. When he described his one-man submarine, the nation (and perhaps the fish, who were given the first view of the model) enjoyed a hearty laugh. Supporters fired back that Ford's ingenuity should be admired, not ridiculed. The phrase "another Ford joke" in the title refers to Ford's peace ship failure and also recalls still earlier jokes about his Model T. The tag line soon became an ironic statement symbolizing that whereas Ford's statements might be jokes to others, when Ford was on the job it was no joke. (From *New York Times,* New York, April 19, 1917.)

to do about that?" asked an officer. "We'll have so many of them," replied Ford, "that we'll use stranded tanks to make a crossing for the following army."[4] The army placed an order for fifteen thousand.

In addition, Ford was also awarded contracts to produce 6,000 Model T ambulances, which he did at a 15 percent discount to American and Allied forces. He produced caissons, over 1,000,000 steel helmets, and submarine detectors for the British navy; lightweight armor plate for tanks; and a design for a robot airplane bomb that anticipated the V-1. Ford joined forces with the Packard

Motor Company and three other manufacturers to produce the Liberty engine, Ford's part being the production of cylinders, of which 415,377 were produced by the end of the war. Later, the Ford organization acquired a contract to produce 5,000 motors, of which 3,940 were delivered before the contract was terminated at war's end.

By now, Ford's reputation had shifted from that of the "peace ship pacifist" to the "fighting pacifist." However, not one single act contributed more greatly to earning Ford this title than his announcement that he would build a submarine patrol boat called the Eagle. The boats (the idea for which was conceived by Ford; Ernest G. Liebold, Ford's personal secretary; and Edward N. Hurley, chairman of the United States Shipping Board, a governmental organization whose sole purpose was to develop ways and means by which ships could be produced at a rapid rate) were supposed to be manufactured at naval or commercial shipyards. The contract was awarded to Ford when it became evident that there were no facilities available elsewhere to build the boats.

Ford not only saw his manufacturing of the Eagle as a chance to serve his country, he also saw it as an opportunity to expand the Rouge River plant, the newest Ford factory, which was destined to replace the outdated Highland Park plant. Ford had wanted to expand the factory for quite a while, but he could not without an attorney for the Dodge brothers checking on his every move. A court injunction had limited company spending to ten million dollars for expansion or renovations. It was far too little money to finance what Ford had in mind for the plant. After perfecting mass production of his cars, "he wanted to master the raw materials that went into cars—the rubber and wood, and, in particular, the coal and iron that made up the steel. He had a vision of a total plant, the ultimate factory, where the raw materials poured in at one end and the finished cars came out at the other."5 Now that the government contract to build the Eagle had been awarded to the Ford Motor Company, Ford could not only do the work he had waited so long to do, he could have the work done at the expense of the U.S. taxpayers. Ford knew that "the Rouge River needed deepening and the marshes needed draining, and as part of the Eagle

With Ford's know-how and backing, our "Liberty Lizzie" would beat back the German U-boats—the poor U-boat never stood a chance, not against the apron-wearing, flag-waving, bloomer-wearing, steaming mad Liberty Lizzie! The image of Liberty Lizzie harks back to the rural and utilitarian aspects of Henry's background. Liberty Lizzie also reminds us that Ford products are reliable and that they stand up against any challenge. (From *Bristol Herald Courier,* Bristol, Virginia, February 2, 1918.)

boat contract, the U.S. government agreed to foot the bill for this."[6] The cost eventually reached $3,500,000. It was suggested, though never promised, that Ford would buy back the plant when the war was over.[7]

The assembly building for the Eagle was over a half mile long and constructed of steel frames. The 350-foot-wide building and 100-foot-tall walls of glass provided room for three moving assembly lines, each capable of accommodating seven boats.

The first Eagle started its trek down the assembly line on May 7, 1918, and was completed by July 10. The secretary of the navy,

Josephus Daniels, predicted that Ford Motor Company would break all shipbuilding records. Ford employees marched down Woodward Avenue lifting banners reading "An Eagle a Day Keeps the Kaiser Away." The *New York Times* wrote that Eagles were being "hatched like flivvers." President Wilson, impressed with Ford's ability to meet deadlines, appointed him to the United States Shipping Board. If Ford could build a ship in two months, he could surely advise others on how to do the same. However, by the time Armistice Day arrived on November 11, 1918, there was only seven Eagles on their way to service, and only two had reached the Atlantic coast.[8]

The Ford Motor Company enjoyed a tremendously positive relationship with the American public throughout most of World War I. It certainly did not hurt that, as David Lewis notes in "Henry Ford in World War I," the Model T itself was cited for "gallantry in action" in a number of battlefield dispatches. For example,

> ten machine-gun-laden T's were used to drive Germans from an entrenched position on the Marne, and the sturdy little car was the only vehicle that could get through to the wounded men during the first five days of fighting in the Argonne Forest. By providing motive power for flat boats, the T saved a detachment of British soldiers from starvation in Africa.[9]

In another instance, General Edmund Allenby attributed the success of the Palestine campaign to "Egyptian laborers, camels, and Ford cars."[10] Even critics of Ford's pacifist views in 1915 and 1916 were silenced. So popular was Ford that he was called "Germany's greatest individual enemy" and "the civilian who is more important to the conduct of the war than any other in the world."[11] This popularity did not go unnoticed by one particular politician in Washington, President Woodrow Wilson, who soon contacted Ford and asked him to run for a seat in the U.S. Senate. Remembering Wilson's lack of support for his peace ship initiative, Ford was reluctant. He remained that way until Wilson sent him a letter that read as follows.

> Mr. Ford, we are living in very difficult times—times when men must sacrifice themselves for their country. I would give anything on

OPEN 'ER UP, HENRY!

This cartoon captures the layperson's view of Ford vividly—if anyone could do the impossible it was Ford and his trusted Model T. If the nation needed boats to win the war and they were not being delivered as contracted, Ford would soon find out why and straighten out the problem. Though Ford never actually did much to speed up production of wartime vessels, the image of Ford being on the job certainly brought a sense of security to American citizens and to American allies. (From *Baltimore Sun,* Baltimore, Maryland, November 17, 1917.)

The Model T was well known for sometimes being stubborn when it came to getting started. Drivers often had to refer to a Model T's manual to figure out what was the matter. This cartoon, which refers to Ford's senatorial boom and the Model T as one and the same, shows the Michigan G.O.P. and the Michigan Democrats taking turns at cranking up Ford for a senatorial race. In saying, "I hope you break your arm," the Michigan G.O.P. representative makes another reference to a Model T characteristic: if a driver was not careful it was easy to break an arm starting the car. In announcing Ford's candidacy for the Senate, the *Bloomington Bulletin* wrote that Ford was "too busy a man for that drowsy body unless he should put motors under the seats and get things moving." (From *Detroit News*, Detroit, Michigan, June 13, 1918.)

At their spring conference in Lansing, Michigan Democrats endorsed Ford, a Republican, for U.S. senator. This action was taken despite the fact that Ford had given no indication that he would accept the nomination if it was tendered at the August primaries. Once again the contrary crank on the Model T becomes a symbol of Henry Ford's stubborn refusal to get started. (From *Newark News*, Newark, New Jersey, August 1918.)

earth if I could lay down this job that I am trying to do, but I must carry on. . . . You are the only man in Michigan who can be elected and help bring about the peace you so desire. I wish you therefore to overcome your personal feelings and interests and make the race.[12]

Ford entered the race as a nonpartisan independent, meaning that he was running as a Democrat and as a Republican. This was not, however, the first time that Ford's name was cast into the political arena. In 1916, he had been a write-in candidate in Michigan for the U.S. presidency, where he defeated Senator Alden Smith on April 1916 by a count of 83,057 to 77,872. And, even though Ford had publicly denied being a candidate or taking his consideration seriously, he almost won a preferential primary in Nebraska and was a write-in candidate on 5,000 ballots in Ohio. At the Republican convention in 1916, Ford received 32 votes on the first call but lost his support by the time the second vote was taken.[13] All of this attention had come Ford's way without him having to lift a finger.

This time around Ford threw his hat into the arena saying, "while I am willing to give whatever time, thought and expense is necessary to do the work well, I am not willing to spend a single cent to get the place."[14]

Democratic papers were supportive; the *Chicago Evening American* and the *New York Journal* ran a half-page ad in the *Detroit Free Press* that read in part that

> every dollar that Henry Ford has made has been made by service to the community, not by combinations creating monopolies and selling products to the public at the highest price, but by competition in price and in excellence that gives the public the greatest amount for the smallest sum.[15]

Republicans and the independent press were critical. The *New York Times* remarked that if elected, Ford "would create a vacancy in the Senate and in the automobile business." The *Grand Rapids Herald* said that the "Senate made laws, not Lizzies."

Ford easily won what would turn out to be the Democratic nomination by more than a four-to-one vote.

His competition in the November 5 election would be Truman

ONE VISION OF THE MICHIGAN SENATORIAL SITUATION

The Michigan G.O.P. elephant cries and the Democratic donkey gallops along as Ford, riding high, controls the reins of both parties. In the background, the front-running Republican, Newberry, works away—steady and true—while from behind the G.O.P. bandwagon is pursued by Chase S. Osborn, a former governor of Michigan and one of Ford's harshest critics. (From *Detroit News,* Detroit, Michigan, July 5, 1918.)

H. Newberry, who was backed by the powerful Republican State Committee. The Newberry family was well known in Michigan. The Newberrys' name headed the *Social Register* generations before the Ford name meant anything to anyone of importance. His family had made its fortune in timber and mining, a large portion of which was invested in the Packard automobile. Newberry had even served in Theodore Roosevelt's cabinet as secretary of the navy. Prior to that he had been a lieutenant commander with a desk job as an aide to a shore admiral. This campaign pitted the pacifist against the war veteran. Newberry also had two sons serving in the armed services, which gave birth to an interesting issue:

When critics questioned Ford's ability to serve in the Senate, Ford responded by saying, "Well, years ago, when I was doing my first tinkering, they said I didn't know anything about automobiles. A year ago they said that I knew all about automobiles, but nothing about building ships. Up to a month ago the riveters turning out those eagle U-boat chasers didn't know a thing about driving rivets, but they are experts today. There is no monopoly of ability, whether statesmanship or rivet-driving" ("Ford Runs for Senate," *New York Evening World*, 4 July 1918). In this cartoon, Ford appears confident enough building a "senatorial candidacy," but one wonders if he is using the right tool. (From *Baltimore Sun*, Baltimore, Maryland, 1918.)

when America entered the war in April 1917, Edsel Bryant Ford, Henry and Clara Ford's only son, was twenty-three years old. With the declaration of war, Edsel's lawyers asked that the draft board exempt Edsel from service. The basis for this request lay in the argument that Edsel would be of greater service to the country supervising Ford munitions production rather than serving in the army or navy.

His request was denied in October 1917, a month after Edsel's first son, Henry Ford II, was born on September 4, 1917. However, a change in regulations moved Edsel into class 2-A, as having dependents, and into class 3-L, as being indispensable to a war industry. Deferment was granted; Edsel did not have to serve in the military.[16]

Ford critics made an issue out of the ruling. The deferment became a key issue in Henry's senatorial campaign. Newspapers in support of Newberry constantly reminded voters that Ford had been successful in keeping his boy out of the trenches and a failure at getting other boys out of the trenches by Christmas. Congressman Nicholas Longworth said that there were seven people in the world who would never have to concern themselves with going to war, those being the six sons of the kaiser and the only son of Henry Ford.

Letters that became feature newspaper articles appealed to the general public not to vote for Ford on the basis of the family's pacifistic bent. One such article ran under the headline "Vote against Ford, Soldiers' Kin Ask." The article read as follows.

> We whose sons have given their lives that we may live, appeal to you in this hour of our grief to vote at the approaching election against Henry Ford for the United States Senate. He has neglected his duty as a citizen; he has failed to defend our country's honor through weak pacifism. . . . He has, through his activities, obtained the release of his son from service, thus leaving him to rest in security and luxury at home while your sons and brothers are facing the enemy in battle and undergoing all the dangers, privations and sufferings of war.[17]

TAKING HIS "DUST.

In the primary election Newberry received 144,963 votes against Ford's 71,800 and Osborn's 47,100. In the Democratic balloting, Ford won by a four-to-one ratio. Even though Newberry's spending was nearing the $150,000 mark, it seemed that Ford's election to the Senate would not be denied, even by the powerful Republican machine of Michigan. Time had indeed proven that a smaller sized Model T could outdo a "gas-guzzler" of the rich. (From *New York Herald,* New York, 1918.)

In Minnesota, the Republican and Democratic Parties joined forces in support of Koute Nelson for the Senate. That the parties could join forces in Michigan was certainly considered and discussed but in the long run never stood a chance of becoming a reality. The differences held between the two parties were too numerous for the idea to gain popularity. Even if the G.O.P. managed to remove the bray from the Democratic donkey it would not be enough to change what the animal stood for. (From *Detroit News,* Detroit, Michigan, June 18, 1917.)

NOTHING LIKE THIS IN HENRY FORD'S WINDOW

In denouncing Edsel Ford's military deferment, the *Detroit Saturday Night* quoted from the *Cloverland Farmer* when it wrote that "if the Ford plant can do without its founder during a congressional session it may well be able to do without his son during the war. Young Ford should take his medicine just like the rest of the boys. He has developed no inventive ingenuity that we have ever heard of that would entitle him to exemption from military duty. We do not wish to be understood as making this criticism in a spirit of enmity nor even unkindness, but only because we like to see fair play. Many thousands of fathers have sons whose services they need at home in shops, stores, plants, and on farms, yet these boys are at the front, fighting for their country." ("What Michigan Thinks of Henry Ford and His Candidacy," *Detroit Saturday Night*, 13 April 1918.)

Ford was also criticized by his former business associate James Couzens. Ford and Couzens had parted ways in 1915 after Couzens objected to Ford's printing of two pacifist articles in the *Ford Times* magazine, an in-house publication with limited circulation. In objecting to Ford's candidacy, Couzens noted Ford's pacifist views and echoed the widespread belief that Ford simply did not have the experience required for the position.

Waiting for the Returns

Seated in the comfort of his fine home and among portraits of Connelly, Hearst, and Schwimmer, as well as among books titled *Gentle Germans, Hauling down the Flag, Why Soldiers Are Crazy,* and *With Mutt and Jeff on the Oscar II,* Ford contemplates his role as a U.S. senator. In a straw poll taken on November 3, 1918, by the *Detroit News,* Ford received 2,069 votes to Newberry's 661. (From *Detroit Saturday Night,* Detroit, Michigan, August 24, 1918.)

Two former presidents, William Howard Taft and Theodore Roosevelt, even wrote letters to Newberry in support of his candidacy. The letters were reprinted in full-page political advertisements in the *Detroit Saturday Night,* a paper popular with the city's social elite and in which Newberry had a small financial investment. Taft viewed Ford as a political pawn who would rubber-stamp any and all Wilson proposals. Theodore Roosevelt's remarks cut deeper, much deeper.

Couzens was one for being prepared in time of war. Here his submarine surfaces long enough to drop off Osborn. Having voiced his views on the Ford candidacy, Couzens now stepped out of the way and let others take their shots. The Ford senatorial boom is symbolized by the four-smokestack steamship, a far different image than that seen during Ford's failed voyage of peace to Europe. (From *Detroit News*, Detroit, Michigan, June 1918.)

The record made by you and your two sons in this war is typical of your whole attitude as a public servant. Both your boys at once entered the navy, and are now on the high seas. You sought employment abroad; when that was refused you, you accepted any position that was offered in which you could render public service.

The nomination of Mr. Ford makes the issue sharp and clear. . . . The issue is infinitely more important than any merely political

While Hughes's and Taft's criticisms of Ford's candidacy were pointed and abrasive, they were nothing compared to the letter written by Theodore Roosevelt in support of Newberry. Note the size and style of Roosevelt's pen as compared to those of the other pens; also note Roosevelt's dress as compared to that of the others. (From *Detroit News*, Detroit, Michigan, November 2, 1918.)

issue. It is the issue of straight Americanism, of straight patriotism, and of preparedness for the tasks of peace and war, as against a particularly foolish and obnoxious type of pacifism, preached in peace and practiced in war. This is the first time in the history of our country in which a candidate for high office has been nominated who has spent enormous sums of money in demoralizing the people of the United States on a matter of vital interest to their honor and welfare. The expenditures on behalf of pacifism by Mr. Ford in connection with the peace ship . . . [were] as thoroughly demoralizing to the conscience of the American people as anything that has ever taken place.

The failure of Mr. Ford's son to go into the army at this time, and the approval by the father of the son's refusal, represent exactly what might be expected from the moral disintegration inevitably produced by such pacifist propaganda. Mr. Ford's son is the son of a man of enormous wealth. If he went to war he would leave his wife and child immeasurably distant from all chances of even the slightest financial strain or trouble, and in his absence would not in the smallest degree affect the efficiency of the business with which he is connected. But the son stays at home, protesting and appealing when he is drafted, and now escaping service. Your two sons have eagerly gone to the front. They stand ready to pay with their lives for the honor and the interest of the American people, and while they thus serve America with fine indifference to all personal cost, the son of wealthy Mr. Ford sits at home in ignoble safety, and his father defends and advises such conduct. It would be a grave misfortune to the country to have Mr. Ford in the Senate when our question of continuing the war or discussing terms of peace may arise, and it would be equally grave misfortune to have him in any way deal with the problems of reconstruction in this country.

Michigan is facing a test, clear-cut and without shadow of a chance for misunderstanding, between patriotism and Americanism on one side and on the other pacifism.[18]

In response to these attacks Ford said nothing, and he spent nothing. His only action was to publicly support women's suffrage and prohibition. Newberry continued spending large amounts of money on his campaign. He hired an army of campaign workers and sent them into ethnic communities throughout the state.

Meanwhile, as the general election drew near, the Republican State Central Committee prepared a document that it published in the *Detroit Free Press* on Sunday, November 3, 1918, under the headline "Henry Ford and His Huns." The paid political advertisement read that

Henry Ford loves Huns too much to be trusted with a seat in the Senate of the United States and help make peace with them. Commander Newberry knows them for what they are and is helping to fight them at every stage of the game. THERE CAN BE ONLY ONE CHOICE FOR WIDE AWAKE AMERICANS IN THIS ELECTION.

The article cited Ford's relationship with Rosika Schwimmer, whom Ford had followed to Europe three years before, and it singled out Ford's failure to fire the head of Ford Motor Company's drafting division, Carl Emde.

"Carl Emde," the article read, "a German alien and sympathizer, is boss of the drafting work on the Liberty Motor at the Ford plant. Henry knows he is a German alien and a German sympathizer, but refuses to take him off that work."

The article cited findings from Charles Evans Hughes, a former justice of the United States Supreme Court, whom President Wilson had appointed "to find out why the production of American aeroplanes [had] been so much delayed when the American soldiers in France needed them so much." In his report to the president, Hughes wrote that "It is possible for one in that department to bring about delays, the cause for which, in view of the multiplicity of drawings involved, it would be difficult to trace."

The article further stated that when Ford's own factory managers reported to Ford that Emde's department was "practically a pro-German institution," Ford reacted by saying that he had heard rumors but that not one single piece of evidence had been presented to him showing Emde's disloyalty to Ford Motor Company or to the United States.[19]

A rebuttal was ready by the next morning, but Ford did not allow the response to be published until he had spoken to Emde in person in order to reassure him of his faith and trust in him. Because of this move, Emde's and Ford's responses to the article did not run until November 5, election day. In his rebuttal, Ford stated that his company's

> policy is to make men, not to break them. In times of panic great injury and injustice are often done to innocent persons and we try to keep our heads. We would not allow injustice to be done to an old trusted and valued employee, even though he was born in Germany.[20]

Accompanying Ford's response was the following quote from U.S. marshal Henry Behrendt, whose job it was to police enemy

Ford complains to Uncle Sam about Newberry's excessive spending, as the steam of his "political aspirations" escapes from his crushed Model T. Newberry, whose steamroller pours out dollar signs, explains his side of the "traffic accident" to the badge-wearing Uncle Sam. Uncle Sam responds, "Oh well, let's see what the judge says!" This cartoon ran a few months after Newberry won the election and Ford accused Newberry of breaking laws governing political spending. (From *Philadelphia Evening Public Ledger*, Philadelphia, Pennsylvania, December 2, 1918.)

infiltration into American industry: "We have had less trouble with enemy aliens in the Ford plant than in any other large plant. If there is any blame with regard to the Ford plant, it should be on the Marshall's office and not on the Ford people. The Ford Motor Company did not employ a single German alien without the permit of the Marshall's office."[21]

In his own defense, Emde wrote "I am not an alien, least of all an alien enemy, but an American citizen. I have given, through the Ford Motor Company, my very best efforts to my country, and believe that a searching investigation of the fact will show that I have in no way betrayed the confidence which Mr. Ford has placed in me."[22]

The rebuttals were published in local newspapers but arrived too late to make the *Detroit Free Press*'s state edition. For this reason thousands of voters went to the polls not having read the case against the damning article. As noted by David L. Lewis in *The Public Image of Henry Ford*, E. G. Pipp, managing editor of the *Detroit News,* "estimated that the failure to reach outside voters before the polls opened cost Ford 10,000 votes. By the time Emde's name had been cleared of the guilt-by-association charges, Ford had lost the first and only major political office he would seek."[23] The final tally was Ford 212,751, Newberry 217,088. A change of fewer than 2,200 votes would have sent Ford to Capitol Hill.

With Ford missing from the fold, the Republicans held the Senate with forty-nine seats to the Democrats' forty-seven. More than that, Ford's loss meant defeat for any chance the United States had of joining the League of Nations.[24] If Ford had been elected, the vote, which stuck to party lines, would have left Vice President Marshall with the decisive ballot. Moreover, with a Ford victory Democrats could have organized Senate committees, but because the Republicans held the majority, anti-Wilson and anti-League Henry Cabot Lodge was made chairman of the Foreign Relations Committee.

Following the election, Ford came on strong, attacking Newberry with a vengeance. Ford accused Newberry of excessive personal spending on his campaign, a violation of federal and state laws concerning campaign expenditures. Ford hired investigators

Truman H. Newberry (*top left corner*) as he appeared in a Grand Rapids federal court on charges of violating the Federal Corrupt Practices Act. Though he was convicted, his sentence of two years and a $10,000 fine was overturned by the Supreme Court. Newberry held on to his seat in the Senate until 1922, when he resigned after Robert La Follette Sr., a Wisconsin Republican, vowed to reopen the case in what was now a Democrat-controlled Senate. (From *Grand Rapids Times,* Grand Rapids, Michigan, February 10, 1919.)

to dig up information on Newberry's spending; he petitioned the Senate to investigate Newberry's spending and asked the Senate to supervise a recount of the November election.

In the end, Ford investigators found no proof of illegal personal spending on Newberry's part. This, however, did not stop Ford from convincing the Department of Justice to seat a special grand jury to investigate the matter further. Newberry was indicted along with 134 other individuals who worked for his primary campaign; each was charged with breaking the Federal Corrupt Practices Act. After all was said and done, Truman Newberry was sentenced to two years in prison and a fine of ten thousand dollars.

Newberry took the case to the United States Supreme Court, which on May 2, 1919, ruled five to four that Congress had exceeded its powers in trying to regulate a state primary election. The ruling did away with Newberry's conviction.

After his acquittal, the Republican held Senate voted to let Newberry keep his seat.

Ford lost the fight, but he never gave up on the battle. In the years to follow he supported candidates that ran against men that had supported Newberry. The first to lose his seat because of Ford's influence was Senator Townsend of Michigan, a Newberry loyalist, who lost in 1922. In the same year, Robert La Follette Sr., a Wisconsin Republican nicknamed "Battling Bob," announced that he planned to reopen the Newberry case. On hearing the news, Newberry turned in his letter of resignation to the governor of Michigan. To stay meant that he would have to stand before a Senate that, with the loss of Townsend, now belonged to the Democrats.

Appointed to take his place in the Senate was none other than James Couzens, who had been elected mayor of Detroit in 1918, the same year Ford had lost to Newberry in the first place. The governor's move surprised everyone. Couzens was not popular because he always told the truth, always said what was on his mind, and never granted any favors—traits no doubt inherited from his old friend and former employer, Henry Ford.

CHAPTER 5

Flexing His Political Muscle:
Henry Ford's Run for the White House

AMERICAN CITIES PROSPERED in the early 1920s, while American farmers found themselves in an economic depression. In the White House, Warren G. Harding was busy proving correct his statement from before his nomination that the Senate was far more to his liking than the presidency. Harding's campaign slogan "Return to Normalcy" turned out to be anything but accurate. His lack of leadership led to the short but severe depression of 1921. By 1922, Republicans lost a number of seats in the congressional election. Harding's administration was quickly losing the people's confidence. With the poor showing of Republicans and his reelection bid looming close, Harding decided to make a speaking tour. He crossed the country and even became the first president to visit Canada and Alaska. It was while he was en route to Alaska that the news regarding the Teapot Dome scandal reached him. A few days later, Harding took ill in Seattle, supposedly of food poisoning. By the time the tour reached San Francisco doctors reported that Harding had pneumonia. Harding would never leave San Francisco alive, dying there on August 2, 1923. In Vermont, where Vice President Calvin Coolidge was enjoying a vacation with his family, his father, who was a notary public, swore him into office in the dining room of the family's farmhouse. It was the first time a father had sworn in a president, and it was the first time the oath of office had been administered by such a minor figure.

For Henry Ford, the early 1920s found business as usual on the financial side with a minor glitch on the production side. His income for 1922 was approximately seventy-five million dollars, and the Model T was rolling out at a rate of 1,300,000 units for the same year. However, Ford had announced in 1922 that he might have to close down Ford plants due to the high cost of coal. Of

A BIG LEAGUE WIRE ACT
IN THE MAIN TENT

During Warren G. Harding's senatorial days in Ohio, his congenial personality made it possible for him to walk a thin line between various factions of the Republican party. This trait, which made him a popular member of Congress, did not translate well into the arena of world politics during his presidential term, where he was viewed as a circus act by the European powers. (From *Boston Post,* Boston, Massachusetts, 1923).

course, this never came to pass, and the Model T kept rolling out as the money rolled in.[1]

The early 1920s also found Ford being mentioned as a possible candidate for the presidency of the United States, yet Ford refusing to acknowledge his interest in the office. With Harding's reputation slipping, the *Detroit Saturday Night* reported that the stage was all set for Henry Ford to become president of the United States. "Whether by act of God or act of Mr. Ford," the paper reported,

> several of the United States senators whom Henry threatened with defeat for voting to seat Senator Newberry have gone down in this election. . . . a democratic landslide has reduced the Republican majority in the senate and left the Republicans with only a precarious

A Senate investigation in 1923 revealed that Secretary of the Interior Albert Fall had persuaded Secretary of the Navy Edwin Denby to transfer government oil reserves at Elk Hills, California, and Teapot Dome, Wyoming, to the Department of the Interior. Fall then leased the reserves to private oil producers E. L. Doheny and Harry Sinclair. These leases were made without competitive bidding. In both cases, Fall received large sums of money for helping to arrange the transfers— $100,000 from Doheny for Elk Hills and $300,000 from Sinclair for Teapot Dome. Fall was part of the "Ohio Gang," a group of Harding's closest friends in high ranking governmental positions. In hearing the breaking news, Harding asked reporters what a president could do when friends betrayed him. (From Library of Congress, Washington, DC, 1923.)

majority in the House of Representatives. . . . Things are coming Henry's way.[2]

Ford-for-President clubs formed throughout the country. Senator Borah, a Republican leader in the U.S. Senate who supported both Republican and Democratic presidents during his thirty-three year tenure, proclaimed the movement "a political revolution, and declared that the Republican and Democratic parties must adopt a 'liberal and conservative policy' or make way for a third party."[3] The *Wall Street Journal* ran an editorial in the autumn

As Ford's popularity as a candidate for president in the 1924 election continued to gain momentum, the country wondered if Ford would run as a Republican or as a Democrat. Ford, who was a Republican, had won the Democratic nomination in his bid for the U.S. Senate in 1918. Here the cartoonist once again joins Henry with his Model T as they race ahead on an independent and unpredictable course. (From *New York Globe*, New York, 1923.)

of 1922 entitled "Why Not Ford for President?" in which the paper threw its support behind the idea of Ford for president. Meanwhile, Ford's nemesis, Senator Newberry, resigned his post as senator, which took care of business that had been on Ford's mind for a number of years. The *Detroit Saturday Night,* owned in part by Newberry, stated that

> the Democrats have had their revenge, and Mr. Newberry has the
> honor of a record as a good fighter and a good loser, a patriot who

THE BIG NOISE IS
DISTURBING THE
PEACE

During Ford's race for the presidency in 1924, his office in Dearborn received a deluge of letters from supporters offering campaign advice. Designs for campaign buttons were submitted, as were slogans such as "Ford Will Give Every Man a Job." A host of loyalists asked for election banners to affix to their flivvers. One individual suggested a parade of Ford cars touring the country proudly displaying Ford pennants and handing out campaign literature. Cartoons during this time often used the Model T and its owner to represent Ford supporters. (From *Boston Post*, Boston, Massachusetts, 1923.)

has suffered untold persecution as a reward for his public service, and a victim of a most contemptible conspiracy between unscrupulous journalism and political savagery backed by unlimited funds.[4]

Not only was there an explosion of interest in Ford as president, there was also an explosion in the number of books about Ford. In total seven books on Ford were published from 1922 to 1923, an astonishing number. Sarah T. Bushnell's *The Truth about Henry Ford*, Rev. William R. Stidger's *Henry Ford: The Man and His Motives,* and James Martin Miller's *The Private Citizen* were extremely flattering. Allan L. Benson's *The New Henry Ford* and E. G. Pipp's *The Real Henry Ford* were not. Henry Ford's spiritual advisor and friend Reverend Marquis wrote *Henry Ford: An Interpretation* at this time as well. This book dispassionately addressed both the good and bad qualities of Henry Ford and pronounced him a complex and often contradictory character. The book, despite its many kind words, hurt Ford. David L. Lewis points out that "The volumes by Marquis and Pipp were, in fact, never available to the public in large numbers, for the Ford organization was fairly successful in buying up and suppressing them."[5]

The seventh book, *My Life and Work,* was an autobiography written by Ford with the assistance of Samuel Crowther. The book, a best-seller around the world, was translated into twelve languages and Braille. Crowther combined material from the regular feature "Mr. Ford's Own Page" in the *Dearborn Independent* and assorted Ford interviews in the book, which spread Ford's philosophy on home and business and set firmly into people's minds the image of the farm boy who did good through hard work and dedication. The book became a "must-read" for English manufacturers and outsold works of fiction in Germany. The book even became a textbook used in Russian universities and technical schools after a number of editorial omissions and revisions. One of the Russian revisions included a statement in the introduction that read "Fordism is a system the principles of which have been known for long, [having been] laid down by Marx."[6]

By the spring of 1923 an article in the *New York Times* read that "Ford looms today a powerful figure on the political horizon." In June and July, *Collier's Weekly* sent representatives to interview individuals in order to conduct a presidential poll. The results of the straw poll showed Ford defeating Harding 88,865 to 51,000.[7]

With sales of the Model T at 1,699,984 for the year 1923, a "Lizzie torchlight parade" stretching from San Francisco through Detroit on to Maine is not as far fetched as this cartoon would suggest. (From *Boston Post,* Boston, Massachusetts, 1923.)

Harding was not concerned with Ford's growing popularity because he had Ford's word that he would not run if Harding was renominated for the presidency.

On August 4, 1923, *Collier's Weekly* published an article titled "If I Were President," an authorized interview by Charles W. Wood. (The interview had actually taken place prior to Harding's passing; thus the issue makes no reference to Harding's death.) Hailed as the "tell-all" story of where Ford stood on the issues of the day, the

With the results of *Collier's Magazine*'s 1923 "straw canvass" of voters in his pocket, a hardworking Ford ponders whether or not to toss his hat into the 1924 presidential ring. The G.O.P. elephant and the Democratic donkey ask, "What's your label??" making reference to the fact that if Ford did run, he also needed to decide if he would run as a Republican or as a Democrat. The hat of the eventual victor, Calvin Coolidge, is not even shown in the presidential ring. It is interesting to note here that the cartoonist chooses to represent Henry in his traditional suit with overalls pulled up over it; it is as if the cartoonist is suggesting that Henry has become all things to all people. (From *Boston Post*, Boston, Massachusetts, 1923.)

article, which had an intimate "fireside chat" feel, painted Ford as a candidate who did not talk like a politician, instead presenting the image of Ford as a person who spoke freely on political subjects. Wood wrote that Ford "talked like a man who had been making a real study of the problems." He was a man who was not ignoring his call to presidential politics but was "trying to find out what it really means. Where does it all belong in the process of social evolution?"

In the article, Ford questioned whether Americans really wanted to make him president or just thought they did. He further commented that

> people think they want to run the Government, when they don't know how. They even think it is a sacred duty to vote, when they haven't got a glimmer of an idea as to what they are voting for. They may even think they are running the Government, but they are not. They are all yanking at it here and there, but they aren't running it; and the more they yank, the more it won't run. There isn't any honor in being stalled. There isn't any honor in anything except usefulness, and usefulness is based upon accurate knowledge of what to do and how to get it done. Suppose I were elected President and didn't know what to do—what kind of honor would I get out of that?[8]

While such a frank statement regarding the general public would have killed the chances of most, if not all, politicians getting elected, the piece clearly showed that Ford had been giving serious consideration to the office of the presidency for quite some time. Most important, the article revealed that if elected, Ford would run the country his way, and if this meant saying things that might hurt or offend a few people, so be it.

Of course, when Ford stated, "I can't say, and no intelligent man can say, what I will do tomorrow" and then concluded the interview by saying, "I know, if the people don't, that that isn't my kind of job. It is as silly to talk of drafting me as it is to try to make me volunteer. I've got a job now—my kind of a job," the article left more questions in its wake than not. Was Henry going to run for president? If so, when was he going to announce his candidacy? Was he going to run as a Republican or as a Democrat? Or was he going to run on a new third party platform?[9]

This cartoon refers to the idea that instead of cheering, "Hip! Hip! Hurrah!" whenever Ford finished a speech, "auto-crats" would simply sound their horns in place of the hip, hip. (From *Boston Post*, Boston, Massachusetts, 1923.)

The answers to these questions started to reveal themselves by mid-October 1923, when Ford did nothing to stop his name from being placed on the presidential preference ballot for the primary elections of the Progressive Party in Nebraska. Ford's intentions also became clear when the head of the Farmer Labor Party of South Dakota stated that Mr. Ford had given his consent to the formation of Ford-for-President clubs in that state.[10] The only thing missing from the picture was Henry's hat in the presidential ring.

Meanwhile, sales of the Model T grew to record numbers, passing the 1,500,000 mark by October 17, 1923. This marked a 60 percent increase from the previous year, meaning that by October 564,774 more had been built than during the previous year. If

This cartoon joked that Ford would launch his own political party in time for the 1924 presidential election. He would have no need for either the Republican or the Democratic Party, not when he could run as a nominee of his "Auto-cratic" Party. (From *Boston Post*, Boston, Massachusetts, 1923.)

Model T sales were any indication, come 1924, Ford would find himself in the White House.[11]

While the idea of Ford for president saw no end to its popularity, stories were published in the country's newspapers in which a number of his associates voiced their concerns or criticized his candidacy. Thomas A. Edison said that he would hate to see Ford as president because he felt it would spoil him. "He's more valuable where he is," Edison flatly pointed out.[12]

WHEN HENRY GETS TO BE PRESIDENT

This cartoon shows us just how much things would change in Washington, DC, if Ford were elected president. In this case, the cartoonist recalls the utilitarian nature of the Model T and its inventor from the many cartoons depicting the various uses of the Model T on the farm. The cartoonist also reminds the public that with Henry Ford on the job things move at a rapid pace and with simplistic order similar to that of his moving assembly line. (From *Des Moines Register*, Des Moines, Iowa, February 21, 1923. Courtesy of the J. N. "Ding" Darling Foundation.)

In a vehement attack, James Couzens responded to a statement issued by Ford during an interview in which Ford berated the fact that Couzens favored allowing 5 percent beer and light wines. In the interview, which Ford gave on October 25, 1923, to a Methodist minister by the name of William Stidger for the *Detroit Times,* Ford said that Couzens

A PHENOMENAL STUNT
FOR A FLIVVER
TO MAKE

The G.O.P. elephant and the Democratic donkey stare down Ford as he honks his horn and prepares to make a leap over them and into the White House. This cartoon is meant to remind Ford and his supporters that without the backing of either the Republican or the Democratic Party, Ford's chances of victory in the 1924 presidential election were almost zero. However, the world knew that there was nothing a Model T or Henry Ford could not accomplish when determined to do so. (From *Boston Post*, Boston, Massachusetts, 1923.)

knows he is wrong about it. Mr. Couzens knows better. He knows that in the Ford Motor plant booze never did anybody any good, and he is taking a backward step when he stands for 5% beer and light wines. Jim Couzens knows better than that. Maybe he feels he is striking a popular chord.

Couzens's rebuttal came during a speech for the Detroit Republican Club in which he said that Ford's remarks on his stance regarding "old-fashioned beer" were in "poor taste from a man so politically ambitious." Couzens further stated that Ford

has never gotten over his defeat as a candidate for United States Senator in Michigan on the Democratic ticket. This man, who has made more unfulfilled promises than any man in America, is now trying to guide or to criticize others. . . . Why does [Ford] refrain from announcing his candidacy? Because he is afraid. He realizes that it would prove just as great a fiasco as his peace ship. . . . Why Ford for President? It is ridiculous. How can a man over 60 years old, who has done nothing except make motors, who has no training, no experi-

In newspapers across the country, a number of articles questioned Ford's ability to serve as president if elected. One paper claimed that if Ford were elected it would be an even bigger joke than his attempt to get the boys out of the trenches by Christmas. Thomas A. Edison went on record as questioning Ford's ability to stand up in front of people and deliver a speech. (From *Boston Post*, Boston, Massachusetts, 1923.)

ence, aspire to such an office? It is most ridiculous. . . . I want to save Ford the greatest humiliation of his career and save the United States Government the humiliation of him as President.[13]

Although Couzens concluded the interview by saying that he loved Ford "as much as it was possible for one man to love another," the sad fact remained that in his opinion Ford was not qualified to be president.

Couzens was not the only one opposing Ford's running for office, Clara Ford, Henry's beloved wife, was also against the idea. The real possibility of Ford being elected crystallized for Clara while she was attending the Daughters of the American Revolution convention in Washington. It was while she was there that she noticed a number of the delegates wearing Ford-for-President buttons. She also took note of the literature circulating the floor in support of Ford. But nothing hit home like the remark made by a delegate in which Clara was described as the ideal first lady. In shock, Clara stood and told the convention chairperson that "Mr. Ford has enough and more than enough to do to attend to his

As the presidential election of 1924 drew near, it seemed that the only way Ford would be denied was if his opponents formed a league with the police to keep his supporters away from the polls. (From *Boston Post,* Boston, Massachusetts, 1923.)

business in Detroit. The day he runs for President of the United States, I will be on the next boat to England." Returning to Fair Lane, the Ford estate, Clara summoned Liebold. On seeing him, Clara said, for right or wrong, "You got us into this! Now get us out!"[14]

In the end, there was nothing Liebold could do to stop Ford from running for president. The only person who could stop Ford was Ford himself.

CHAPTER 6

Ford and Muscle Shoals: The Muscle in Ford's Bid for the White House

PERHAPS NO OTHER EVENT strengthened Ford's claim to the White House in 1924 more than his bid on July 8, 1921, for a government project commonly referred to as Muscle Shoals. A government-supported undertaking made possible by the National Defense Act of 1916, Muscle Shoals existed for the sole purpose of producing nitrate for use in explosives for World War I. Unfortunately, by the time the two nitrate plants were completed in 1918 the war was over. The plants, however, were still viewed by farmers as money well spent because the nitrate produced by the plants could now be used in manufacturing fertilizers. Prior to the approval of the Muscle Shoals project, America depended on nitrate supplies shipped in from Chile. During the war the great fear was that German submarines would sink shipments, thus leaving America with no nitrate supplies for use in producing explosives. However, the fear now was that the Muscle Shoals installation cost too much money to keep open. So far the United States had invested eighty-five million dollars in the project, and yearly upkeep ran as high as three hundred thousand dollars. Congress debated: Should the project remain idle? Should the Wilson Dam, which was under construction, be completed? Should fertilizers be produced? If so, what would happen to private business that also produced fertilizers? Should Muscle Shoals be sold to a private company? Whatever the outcome, scrapping the project altogether was not an option.

While Congress debated the subject, Secretary of War John Weeks announced that he would recommend the completion of the Wilson Dam if any private company leased Muscle Shoals. The

The original caption accompanying this sketch of Muscle Shoals read, "This picture, upon the spot, shows, as it is today, the Wilson Dam, biggest in the world.
Nearly a mile long and 137 feet high, it will have an ultimate capacity of 600,000
horsepower and is only a part of the vast development of the Tennessee River.
Work upon it was begun during the war and, except for one interval of inaction
some years ago, Government engineers have been employed upon it ever since."
(From *New York Times Magazine Section*, New York, April 27, 1924.)

only provision was that the leasing company had to be willing to
turn over to the government a return on its investment.

Henry Ford took the government up on its offer to lease Muscle Shoals and submitted a bid on July 8, 1921. His terms were
clearly laid out and were published in a number of newspapers
and magazines. In the following, found in the *Michigan Business*

Farmer dated July 23, 1921, Ford's proposal is clearly outlined. It reads as follows.

1. The government agrees to complete both Dam No. 2 and the Wilson Dam at an estimated cost of $28,000,000. This includes the installation of locks, turbines, power houses and all power equipment.

2. The Ford Company will then lease this entire power outfit for a period of 100 years and pay the government annually a sum equal to six per cent of the $28,000,000 and in addition a sum each year sufficient to extinguish within the 100 years the entire cost of the dams, estimated to be in the neighborhood of $40,000,000. Mr. Ford also makes certain proposals to arrange for the maintenance and upkeep of the structures during the period of the lease.

3. The Ford Motor Company offers to purchase all the nitrate plants, equipment, lands, quarries and other property in connection with the plants for a sum set at $5,000,000.

4. To convert and operate the large nitrate plant for the production of fertilizers of various kinds, and to keep it in readiness to produce nitrates for explosives for the government in case of war.

5. In order to insure that fertilizers will be produced at lowest possible costs and sold to farmers at low prices, Mr. Ford binds himself to limit the profits to not more than 8 per cent and to create a board made up of representatives of the large farm organizations, and other interested bodies, to meet with representatives of the plant, have access to all books and records, and determine whether or not this maximum is being observed.

    By proper engineering developments the power made available at the dam would eventually far exceed that needed for fertilizer production and Mr. Ford is to have this for his manufacturing uses. A large use of this addition [*sic*] power is necessary in order to keep down the cost of the power used in fertilizer production.[1]

Prior to Ford's bid, the Muscle Shoals project meant little to

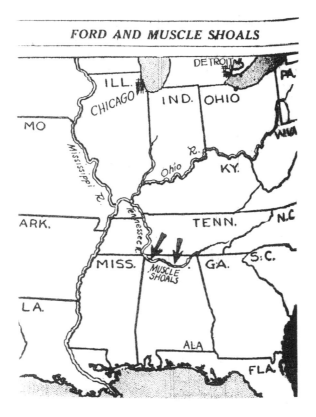

Artist's rendering of Muscle Shoals that ran in *Chicago Daily Tribune*, April 4, 1921, under the heading "Ford and Muscle Shoals." A number of maps of this type ran in urban newspapers. Their purpose was to educate the public as to the location of Ford's latest interest. Under this particular map the caption read in part "Henry Ford has offered to lease the Muscle Shoals works for a period of 100 years, as well as purchasing the nitrate plant and completing other plants. Ford would pay $5,000,000 outright and assume an annual obligation of $1,500,000." (From *Chicago Daily Tribune*, Chicago, Illinois, April 16, 1921.)

the average American living in an urbanized area. Most Americans were not even aware of the location of Muscle Shoals. The program had to be introduced, along with Ford's interest in the property, starting with the geographical location of the site. The *Detroit News* did just that on December 12, 1921, when it introduced the area and the government project behind it. The story read as follows.

> Muscle Shoals is a waterpower site on the Tennessee River, in Northern Alabama.
>
> The Tennessee River, born among countless cascades and springs in the Smoky Mountains, the most southerly range of the Alleghenies, flows down past Chattanooga, then winds south through gorge and meadow as far as Decatur in Northern Alabama, then turns almost north, up through Alabama, Tennessee and Kentucky until, after innumerable windings, it empties its flood into the Ohio River, below Cincinnati, a course of approximately 1,200 miles.
>
> In Lauderdale County, adjacent to the Tennessee line, the bluffs that confine the course of the river are crowned by two cities—on the north bank, Florence, a city of 10,000; on the south, Sheffield, a city of about 6,000 population. Just at this point, and for miles above and below, the bed of the river is jagged with rocks and boulders. When the river is low, the rocks can be seen; when the river is high, their presence is made known by the violent eddies and tumbling of the water. This is Muscle Shoals.[2]

The river at this point was just under a mile wide. In the river were two islands: Patton's Island, directly opposite the city of Florence, and Jackson's Island, just upstream. The government's plan called for damming the river, with a man-made route allowing passage around the power works. The plan called for three dams. Dam 1 would run from the western tip of Patton's Island to the mainland; dam 2, from the mainland straight across the river to about the middle of Jackson's Island; and dam 3, across the river's full width about sixteen miles above dams 1 and 2. Dam 3 was to be known as the Wilson Dam—it was to be the great work of the project. At this point in time, dam 1 was finished, dam 2 was about two-thirds completed, and work on dam 3 was just getting under way.

The government was trying to find someone who could take over the whole project and operate it when the dams were completed and power could be developed. At the time of the announcement, Henry Ford was the only party that made the government a constructive proposition—a proposition offering to pay something for the project. There had been other offers, but all

The situation in the Tennessee Valley was not new to Washington. In 1905 President Theodore Roosevelt had vetoed a bill that would have allowed a private company to build a dam at Muscle Shoals. By 1907, the idea of building a dam on the river subsided completely when the National Waterways Committee ruled that the Tennessee River was too powerful to be tamed by a private company, suggesting instead that a system be developed that provided management of the river as a unit. Ford's proposal offered the area renewed life and a promise of prosperity. (From *Montgomery News*, Montgomery, Alabama, February 14, 1923.)

were on the basis that the government had to turn over the property for nothing against loss for a term of years.

If Congress gave the lease to Mr. Ford, he intended to manufacture steel, aluminum, and nitrates—the latter to give the American farmer a very efficient artificial fertilizer at a cheap price. When Congress would act on Ford's bid was anyone's guess.

What the *Detroit News* did not mention in its description of the Muscle Shoals project was that the population in the area was well over four million, with a large percentage of them farmers. Water for the river came from the southern Appalachian Mountains, where rainfall averaged over eighty inches a year. This created a flooding problem for the 650 miles that ran from Knoxville, Tennessee, to Paducah, Kentucky. When the river drained it took with it the topsoil. Bearing the brunt of this natural occurrence was the farmer. A study of the area had pointed out that "as a result, most of the farmers were in poverty, unable to support good schools, hospitals, or roads. Only two percent of the farms had electricity, while most of the people lived in overcrowded, unsanitary houses, and lacked proper food and clothing."[3] In part, Ford's offer had the potential of helping these farmers out of poverty.

In newspaper interviews Ford spoke about his vision of a city in the area that was seventy-five miles long and fifteen miles wide. The streets would have names mirroring those of popular Detroit streets, such as John R. and Woodward. The city would be so large that it would surpass Detroit, which at the time was one of America's fastest growing cities. He described the project as one of the greatest undertaken by industrial America. The power generated from the river would travel through miles of lines, bringing affordable electricity to manufacturing plants, homes, machinery, and farmers. One Ford biographer pointed out that "people had such faith in Ford that his words created a stampede to the Tennessee Valley. Real-estate went sky-high, orchards were planted, truck farms laid out, cattle ranches built and stocked to supply the inhabitants of the new wonder city."[4]

Ford's bid received support from prominent individuals throughout the South. Bankers, manufacturers, and farmers agreed that Ford's interests in Muscle Shoals would "mean the

While the Committee Sleeps on the Ford Offer

The committee appointed to consider offers made on Muscle Shoals consisted of Secretary of War John W. Weeks, Secretary of the Treasury Andrew W. Mellon, and Herbert Hoover of the Commerce Department. Weeks, a prime mover in initiating policy, never publicly favored Ford's proposal. Mellon opposed the development because it threatened his investments in aluminum, and Hoover was simply unable to make up his mind. Ford's bid found support with the American Federation of Labor, the National Grange, the Farmer's Union, and the Farm Bureau Federation. By the time this cartoon made its appearance Ford's offer was nearly a year old. In looking at the situation the *Philadelphia Bulletin* wrote "If Henry Ford wants to get the Muscle Shoals project out of the congressional trenches by Christmas, let him try." (From *Flint Journal,* Flint, Michigan, April 22, 1922.)

rehabilitation of a vast stretch of country which, for more than a half-century, has lain all but sterile agriculturally, producing but a minimum of its possible yield and, industrially, has had only meager development."[5]

"We hope Ford will get Muscle Shoals," said one Birmingham banker, "because if he comes down here he will undo what Sherman did. Ford will make it possible for us to help ourselves."[6]

At the time of his original proposal Ford said, "My purpose in taking over Muscle Shoals is not to benefit us or our business in Detroit or any other part of the country—my one purpose is to do a certain thing that will benefit the whole world. . . . We can here do an epochal thing—literally, I mean it—an epochal thing. We shall eliminate war from the world." Here we see a stately Ford more in keeping with the image of a statesman than that of an auto baron being supported by the giant hand of the public. The many popular calls for Ford to run for office helped add this new variation on the Ford image to the cartoonists' choice of renderings. (From *Detroit Times,* Detroit, Michigan, 1923. Approved by Mark Silverman, Publisher and Editor. Reprinted with permission from The Detroit News.)

Ford sat patiently waiting to hear from Weeks and Congress, whose job it was to consider all bids before the Senate and the president. When word did not come, Ford went on the offensive. He went on record accusing "the fertilizer trust, the power and chemical interests of Wall Street, the money brokers, and other interests that fear to have Muscle Shoals developed along lines that will serve all the people most" of circulating literature to Weeks and Congress "that grossly misrepresents the facts."

Ford, however, laid the blame for a lack of progress on Weeks when he went on to state that

STILL WAITING FOR THE MAN TO TIE THE KNOT

While Congress examined recommendations on bids submitted to Weeks, Mellon, and Hoover, the American public interested in the subject of Muscle Shoals waited impatiently. Many times during the Muscle Shoals affair, Ford, when up against the big politicians, is reduced to labels symbolizing his actions, such as here, where "Ford's Offer" is displayed on the groom's coattails, while Ford stands waiting. (From *Albion Recorder,* Albion, Michigan, May 12, 1922.)

This is not a political matter to be jockeyed about. Why doesn't Secretary Weeks take it or leave it, "yes" or "no," as he would a private business matter. I mean that now, after six months, he is still asking what appear to me as irrelevant questions and delaying the settlement of this matter.[7]

At the same time, Ford defended charges that he could not make fertilizer at Muscle Shoals on a profitable commercial basis.

"FORD: 'Gimme that'

In the cartoon, Henry Ford is once again drawn up as the diminutive David figure fighting another Goliath. Only this time the Goliath is not Mars but Uncle Sam, and Ford sounds more like a greedy capitalist than a peace-loving citizen as he shouts "Gimme that" to the giant. (From *Detroit Sunday Times*, Detroit, Michigan, May 1923. Approved by Mark Silverman, Publisher and Editor. Reprinted with permission from The Detroit News.)

He did this by confidently stating that "Thomas A. Edison says we can."

"I'm not a chemist," Ford shot at his critics, "but Edison has been down there and knows every detail of this proposition. He is working on this thing right now in his laboratory at East Orange. He says that with Muscle Shoals we can give the American people a better fertilizer at a much lower price than they have ever had before."

Ford's remarks were based on his recent visit to Muscle Shoals with Edison in early December 1921 to "study the possibilities of the waterpower site and nitrate plant."[8]

Ford was not alone in his wait to hear from Weeks. By April 9, 1922, Congress was considering offers from no less than three additional parties: the Alabama Power Company, Fredrick Engstrum, and Charles Parsons. Congress was further slowed by the submission of a bill by Congressman George William Norris, a Republican from Nebraska, that called for "a Government owned and operated corporation to be conducted under the supervision of three directors." The president would appoint the panel. The sole purpose of the committee would be the development of the nitrate and waterpower projects at Muscle Shoals, Alabama.[9]

Norris's proposal gained support from Couzens, who "argued persuasively that neither Ford nor any other private individual ought to have the government-owned nitrate and power development, but that it should be held by the government for the benefit of the public."[10]

While Ford's offer labored in Congress for the better part of two years, his popularity as a potential candidate for president of the United States grew beyond the South and the Midwest to include the West. The *New York Times* reported that

> there is no doubt that Mr. Ford has developed remarkable strength as a Presidential possibility in the West, particularly among farmers. A number of Republican Senators have testified to this sentiment in their States. Many farmers, dissatisfied with existing economic conditions and inclined to be angered at the Republican Party, have the belief that Ford, being a remarkably successful business man, will be able to run the Government with equal success.

The Party Line.

Ford's bid for Muscle Shoals never received an endorsement from a Republican congressman or senator. When Ford's proposal finally won approval in the House of Representatives on March 10, 1924, it was only because those present voted along party lines. In this cartoon, Ford is once again reduced to a word on a bell. On one hand, the telephone bells symbolize Ford's lack of political power and, on the other, Ford's determination not to go away. (From *Montgomery News*, Montgomery, Alabama, 1923.)

The promise of Mr. Ford that if he gets control of the Government nitrate plant at Muscle Shoals he will furnish cheap fertilizer to farmers has had a marked effect in creating Ford sentiment in agricultural sections.[11]

Ford's bid was not the only contributing factor to his growth in popularity. With the death of President Harding and the breaking news of the Teapot Dome scandal, Ford's chances of *not* landing in the White House were indeed very slim. The only thing that could stop Ford now was Ford himself—a very unlikely move, yet a move that Ford made on December 19, 1923, when he bowed out of the race by issuing a statement announcing his support of Calvin Coolidge for president.

"Mixed reactions followed, with many congratulating Ford for

Following his meeting with Calvin Coolidge, Ford was accused of striking a deal: he would get Muscle Shoals and Coolidge would get the White House. This cartoon utilizes the image of Ford as "the wholesale Santa Claus" back at his old tricks, while the leader of the Progressive Party gives chase hoping to win favor with Coolidge before it is too late. (From *Boston Post,* Boston, Massachusetts, 1923.)

bowing out of the race, while others feared America had lost its chance to elect its greatest president."[12] A disappointed Minnesotan believed Ford "had chickened out, leaving us who thought we had a leader for the great Armageddon, the fight between right and wrong, between man and money, between freedom and slavery, between Christ and Satan. We now wonder if we haven't been worshipping a Tin God."[13]

In the newspapers, articles claimed that Ford and Coolidge had struck a deal following a visit to the White House by Ford on December 3: Coolidge would get the White House; Ford would get Muscle Shoals. Newspapers also turned to Coolidge's speech on December 6 before Congress "in which he advised the sale of Muscle Shoals. This, it was disclosed, was interpreted by members of the Committee on Agriculture as being favorable to Mr. Ford."[14]

While the dealings of Ford and Coolidge made headlines, Congress was finally down to the work of voting on Ford's proposal. Talk on the congressional floor was brutal. Representative Burton, a Republican from Ohio, vigorously attacked the Ford offer, which he described as "utterly inadequate."

"There are possibilities in this situation," Burton said, "which might make Teapot Dome look like a mere bagatelle."

Chairman Snell followed Burton's lead, adding that acceptance of Ford's offer would give Ford "undisputed possession of an immensely valuable waterpower belonging to the nation, built by the nation's money and built mainly for the purpose of the national security in time of war. This proposition has Teapot Dome beaten a hundred ways in giving away Government property, and before you are through with it, it will be a bigger scandal."

Representative James, a Republican from Michigan, supported Ford's offer, saying, "this is not a fight between members of Congress as to the future of Muscle Shoals, but a fight between the power and fertilizer trusts and those who believe in furnishing farmers cheap fertilizer and of being prepared to manufacture nitrates for explosive in time of war."[15]

On March 10, 1924, the House of Representatives voted to approve Ford's bid. While Ford celebrated his victory and prepared to face the Senate, a Senate in which his old friend Couzens

As Congress prepared to vote on Ford's bid for Muscle Shoals, this cartoon served to remind congressmen and their constituents that if Henry Ford or "allied power companies" won the lease on Muscle Shoals, it would be a great financial loss to taxpayers. An assortment of critics estimated the government's investment in Muscle Shoals at $105,000,000, for which Ford would only have to pay $5,000,000 to obtain. Note that the words "Ford bid," while on top of the stack, are diminutive in comparison to Uncle Sam's image. (From *Lansing Capital News,* Lansing, Michigan, January 16, 1924.)

was reporting that Ford had used Muscle Shoals "more for political purposes than from a desire to manufacture nitrates for farmers,"[16] news broke that evidence existed substantiating the claim that Coolidge and Ford had formed a pact in regard to Muscle Shoals. The evidence came in the form of a telegram: a telegram that was sent to Ford's private secretary, Ernest G. Liebold, by a Washington correspondent named James M. Miller.

THE DOG IN THE MANGER

In this editorial cartoon, the artist uses the expression "dog in the manger" when referring to those opposing Ford's plans. The phrase "dog in the manger" means, according to *Merriam Webster's Collegiate Dictionary*, tenth edition, "a person who selfishly withholds from others something useless to himself." The phrase originated from a fable written in 1573, in which a dog keeps an ox from eating hay that he does not want for himself. In this cartoon, favorable to Ford's bid, the artist gives us a strong image of Henry towering over his opponents. He is bundled in his signature fur coat, smiling securely at the advancing canine. Ford's reputation for no-nonsense dealings with politicians and bankers is being drawn into service here. (From *Dallas Morning News*, Dallas, Texas, January 18, 1922.)

Hearing of the telegram, the senatorial committee subpoenaed copies of the telegram.[17] In the telegram Miller had written Liebold that

> In private interview had with President Coolidge this morning he said incidentally: "I am friendly to Mr. Ford, but wish some one would convey to him that it is my hope that Mr. Ford will not do or say anything that will make it difficult for me to deliver Muscle Shoals to him, which I am trying to do." While president didn't say so, am sure Weeks has been in consultation with President this morning in view of Mr. Ford's reported interview today's papers [sic].[18]

On the stand, Liebold denied that Miller was an employee of Mr. Ford. He further stated that

> none of Mr. Miller's telegrams were taken seriously. Mr. Miller occasionally contributed articles to *The Dearborn Independent* and quite frequently sent telegrams to Dearborn. But, if the telegram advising Mr. Ford to cease criticism of Secretary Weeks was ever received, it was regarded as of no practical importance and no attention was paid to it. No such message was ever given to Mr. Ford. It is quite possible that we did receive a telegram, as we frequently were in receipt of wires from many sources, but I have no recollection of it.[19]

In the end, Miller responded that a man in his position could not afford to have a controversy with the president of the United States. "But," he concluded, "I want to say that I quoted the President correctly in my telegram. Perhaps, however, Mr. Coolidge has forgotten, because in the thousands of duties that demand his attention it may be difficult for him to recall one of many conversations."[20]

In regard to the acquisition, and in putting the matter to rest, Coolidge issued a statement that read, in part,

> The Government is undertaking to develop a great water power plant known as Muscle Shoals, on which it has expended many million dollars. The work is still going on. Subject to the right to retake in time of war, I recommend that this property, with a location for auxiliary steam plant and rights of way, be sold. This would end the present burden of expense and should return to the Treasury the largest prices possible to secure.

Tired of waiting and of the politics involved in securing Muscle Shoals, Ford withdrew his offer to lease the property on October 15, 1924. Dejected farmers urged him to stay in the fight. One woman wrote "We know you don't need Muscle Shoals, but Muscle Shoals needs you." Eastern aristocrats still felt that granting Ford Muscle Shoals "would have been the biggest real estate swindle since Adam and Eve were euchred out of the Garden of Eden" (Reynold M. Wik, *Henry Ford and Grass-roots America*). With Ford's offer withdrawn, the area did not reach its full potential until 1933 with the establishment of the Tennessee Valley Authority. (From *Montgomery News*, Montgomery, Alabama, 1923.)

While the price is an important element, there is another consideration even more compelling. The agriculture of the nation needs a greater supply and lower cost of fertilizer. . . .

I have never said I was trying to deliver Muscle Shoals to Mr. Ford or to any one else. I do not think his favor is for sale. I wanted him to have his proposal fairly considered. My mind was made up when Mr. Ford called on me on December 3, and at that time my message was already written, printed and had been sent to the press for five days. My message went out November 28, five days before Mr. Ford came to see me. I expected there would be other bids, and wanted all of them considered on their merits.

This question ought to be decided on its merits. I have no other method of dealing with it. The Congress should have none.[21]

Tired of it all, Ford withdrew his bid on October 15, 1924. His *Dearborn Independent* painted a David and Goliath story reminiscent of Ford's portrayal during the peace ship voyage. Ford's efforts to help the farmer, the laborer, the little man had been "blocked by bankers, by fertilizer trusts, by utility companies, and by the nefarious financiers of Wall Street."[22]

In the end, Coolidge became president, Ford continued making the Model T, and Clara had Henry just where she always preferred him, at Fair Lane.

As for Muscle Shoals and the rest of the over forty-two thousand acres making up the Tennessee River Valley, they would have to wait until the Tennessee Valley Authority was established in 1933 before they would ever start to reach their full potential.

CHAPTER 7

Claim of Ignorance:
Ford, Jews, and the Sapiro Trial

ON DECEMBER 30, 1918, Henry Ford submitted his resignation as president of Ford Motor Company. The reason he gave was "to devote my time to building up other organizations with which I am connected." One of the organizations to which Ford was connected was the *Dearborn Independent.* Acquired in November 1918, the *Independent,* as it was known at the time of purchase, was published in Dearborn, Michigan. The move was classic Henry Ford; here was one of the richest men in the world, a man that could afford to buy a newspaper with a national reputation but who instead bought a local newspaper with a sound base of one thousand subscribers. Ford's plans for the newspaper were grand. He visualized the *Dearborn Independent* being "distributed to newsstands across the country—a homely, 'plain-folks' publication that would sell so well it could get itself racked up alongside the *New York Times* and the *Wall Street Journal.*"[1]

After the purchase, Ford moved his newspaper to the tractor plant he had built across the street from Fair Lane. The paper would be run in similar fashion to the production of the Model T: a story would start at one end of the assembly line with nothing more than a headline; as the article moved down the way, one writer would report on the facts, another would add humor, another editorial comment, and so on, until the article came off the assembly line a finished product.[2]

E. G. Pipp, the newspaper's managing editor, whom Ford had lured away from the *Detroit News,* convinced Ford that while the idea was a good one, it could be simplified further if each writer contributed a humorous article, a political article, an editorial, pictures, cartoons, and so on, until the newspaper was finished and rushed off to the composing room in preparation for printing. Ford approved of the plan: here was efficiency at its best. That this was the way all newspapers operated was of little consequence to Ford.

Ford appointed himself president, Clara vice president, and Edsel secretary treasurer. Ford also gave himself the privilege of writing his own column, "Mr. Ford's Own Page." The column would give Ford an opportunity to share his opinions on big business, Wall Street, and bankers. A decision was also made not to accept advertisements. In this way, Ford would not be at anyone's mercy when voicing his opinions on any subject. William J. Cameron, a journalist that Pipp had brought over from the *Detroit News,* was assigned to actually write the articles. Ford shared his insights, and Cameron put them down on paper.

The *Augusta Journal* surmised that "Henry Ford has turned away from the automobile business to publish a weekly newspaper. Of course this radical change at this time of life is for the purpose of acquiring a competence for his chimney-corner days."[3] The *Brooklyn Eagle* wrote that "for Proprietor Henry Ford the *Dearborn Independent* is an admirably descriptive newspaper title, and his 'Great Expectations' are hinted at by the selection of Mr. E. G. Pipp, as editor. What the Dickens his great expectations are the world cannot guess at present."[4] The *Los Angeles Times,* however, knew exactly what Ford was up to. Their editorial cartoonist drew up a good old hardworking "Hennery," with pencil in ear, dressed in his usual formal attire, who would now "run the whole she-bang!" Powered by the strong engine of his Model T, the world would turn in a new direction—from north to south—with the obedient son, Edsel, at the wheel. The *Detroit Times,* in typical fashion, supported Ford by writing "move over please, and make a place for Henry Ford on the editorial tripod. The new volunteer is thrice welcome. If he does as much good with his journal of civilization as he has with his factories, bank, school, farm, and hospital, the world will be better."[5]

The *Dearborn Independent* debuted on January 11, 1919, with the following purpose printed on the front page:

In unveiling his *Dearborn Independent,* Ford stated, "I am very interested in the future, not only of my own country, but of the whole world and I have definite ideas and ideals that I believe are practical for the good of all, and intend giving them to the public without having them garbled, distorted, or misrepresented." One critic described the *Dearborn Independent* as dull, "as tranquil as a peace ship upon a painted ocean . . . the *Oscar II* of the becalmed journalistic main." (Ford and critic both quoted in David L. Lewis, *The Public Image of Henry Ford.*) (From *Los Angeles Times,* Los Angeles, California, November 1918.)

Into the new time with all its prophetic forces, *The Dearborn Independent* comes to put its shoulder to the car of social justice and human progress.

This paper owes its establishment to Henry Ford's desire to serve the new freedom of the future.[6]

The first issue did not live up to "great expectations." Stories ran in regard to the League of Nations, Postmaster General Burleson's support of government-controlled telephone and telegraph systems, and Secretary of the Navy Daniels's contradictory stance on preparedness and disarmament. There was also a fictional war story entitled "When Peace Came to St. Raphael." Filling out the rest of the paper were cake recipes, dress patterns, and filler material aimed at a rural audience. Ford's feature consisted of "the frontier 'philosophy of scarcity.' . . . We must work incessantly. We must produce—things, more things." This philosophy was voiced in a variety of ways in columns to come. For example, one column read "It is a bad thing to 'make business' by making things that serve no use," while another read "I would rather that a man made a million ploughs than that he made a million dollars. If he gets the money making the ploughs, well and good—it will help him to make more and better ploughs and so increase the production of food."

Sarcastically, the *Detroit Saturday Night,* never a friend to Ford, observed that it was the "best weekly ever turned out by a tractor plant."[7]

The *Dearborn Independent* remained a lackluster newspaper during its first year. Ford used it as a forum to denounce big business, bankers, and Wall Street. Prohibition was regarded as a war won. Subscriptions grew to 56,688, but it was not enough to show a profit. Ford ended the first year $284,000 in the red. By March 13 of the following year there were only 26,000 subscribers left.[8] Something had to change, not because the paper was losing money but because the paper was not growing in national stature as Ford had hoped.

In order to increase circulation Pipp suggested that the paper hold a contest for writers of fiction. The winners would be published. Joseph O'Neill, a staff journalist, after "a careful study of the reasons the *Independent* was not a success," wrote Liebold, Ford's personal secretary, suggesting that the magazine

find an evil to attack, go after it and stay after it . . . name names, and tell actual facts. . . . PUSSY-FOOTING and being afraid to hurt

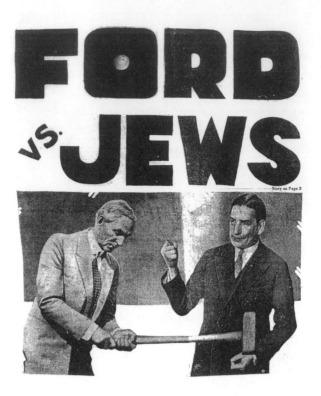

The original caption for this drawing read "Sapiro Sues Henry Ford for One Million Dollars for Jewish Attacks: Because of his attacks against Aaron Sapiro (*right*) and other noted Jews, Henry Ford (*left*) must appear in court next Tuesday. He is being sued in Detroit for $1,000,000 libel damages because of attacks on Sapiro in the *Dearborn Independent*. Ford charged that Sapiro and other Jews were engaged in a huge conspiracy to control the farms and finances of America." So ignored was the *Independent's* attack on Jews that a staff member responsible for subscriptions charged that the popular press was "maintaining what may be termed a 'conspiracy of silence' insofar as mention of the *Dearborn Independent* series . . . is concerned" (H. W. Roland letter to E. G. Liebold, September 4, 1920; Henry Ford Museum and Greenfield Village Research Library). Coverage of the Jewish related articles was to remain virtually nonexistent until the filing of Sapiro's lawsuit, which claimed defamation of character. It is interesting to note that in the original caption for this cartoon the reader had to be told who was Ford and who was Sapiro. (From *New York Daily Mirror*, New York, March 11, 1927.)

people will keep us just where we are if not send us further down the ladder. . . . If we get and print the right sort of stuff, ONE SINGLE SERIES may make us known to millions. A succession of series of FEARLESS, TRUTHFUL, INTERESTING, PLAIN-SPOKEN articles, if properly handled . . . will make a lasting reputation. . . . LET'S HAVE SOME SENSATIONALISM.[9]

O'Neill's report also warned that some people might be offended and then countered by asking, "But shouldn't we offend people? If we are going to tell only *pleasant* truths, we might as well consolidate with the *Christian Herald.* If this magazine is ever going to get anywhere at all, it will have to FIGHT."[10]

By April 17, 1920, Pipp was gone as the editor of the paper. He would go on to start the *Pipp Weekly,* and he eventually became editor of the *Detroit Saturday Night,* the publication most outspoken against Ford at the time. Pipp's departure, however, did not signal change, because for the next four weeks the paper looked the same as those that had come before. Then on May 22, 1920, everything about the *Dearborn Independent* changed. The paper shrank to half its original size, illustrations and articles from the various "departments" were gone, and an article regarding Jews made its appearance. These changes were a clear indication as to why Pipp had resigned as editor. The article regarding Jews was published on the front page. The headline to the story read "The International Jew. The World's Problem." A paragraph under the headline introduced the reader to the topic at hand. Taken word for word from *The New International Encyclopedia,* the introductory paragraph read as follows.

Among the distinguishing mental and moral traits of the Jews may be mentioned: distaste for hard or violent physical labor; a strong family sense and philoprogenitiveness; a marked religious instinct; the courage of the prophet and martyr rather than of pioneer and soldier; remarkable power to survive in adverse environments, combined with great ability to retain racial solidarity; capacity for exploitation, both individual and social; shrewdness and astuteness in speculation and money matters generally; an Oriental love of display and a full appreciation of the power and pleasure of social position; a very high average of intellectual ability.[11]

The article that followed claimed that there was "a race, a part of humanity which has never yet been received as a welcome part, and which has succeeded in raising itself to a power that the proudest Gentile race has never claimed—not even in Rome in the days of her proudest power."[12]

In addition to the articles, a detective agency was set up in New York City for the sole purpose of digging up negative information on Jews. "The agency's prize acquisition was *The Protocols of the Wise Men of Zion,* a document which supposedly emanated from a secret conclave of world Jewish leaders."[13] The *Protocols* had been proven as a forgery years prior to Ford discovering them; the Jewish community did not understand Ford's obsession with the document. Written by the czarist spy, Serge Nilus, the *Protocols* "had been published by the Russian government in 1905 in order to divert the revolutionary activities of the Russian people into anti-Semitic channels."[14] Ford apparently believed that the *Protocols* was a real historical document.

In an article titled "Does a Jewish World Program Exist?" with the subheading "An Introduction to Documents Which Are Now Being Circulated as the Jewish World Program," the *Dearborn Independent* showed its ignorance with the following statement.

> Whosoever was the mind that conceived them possessed a knowledge of human nature, of history and of statecraft which is dazzling in its brilliant completeness, and terrible in the objects to which it turns its power. Neither a madman nor an intentional criminal, but more likely, a super-mind mastered by devotion to a people and a faith could be the author, if indeed one mind alone conceived them. It is too terribly real for fiction, too well-sustained for speculation, too deep in its knowledge of the secret springs of life for forgery. . . . The *Protocols* are a World Program—there is no doubt anywhere of that.[15]

The articles left Jews and Gentiles bewildered as to why Ford suddenly took this stance. Dr. Leo M. Franklin, a rabbi at the Temple Beth-El in Detroit who was a close friend of Ford and a staunch Ford supporter since the five-dollar days, wrote a letter to Ford questioning his involvement. The letter read as follows.

> There is no man either in public life or within the circle of my acquaintance for whom I entertain a higher personal regard than for

you, nor is there one of whose sense of justice I am more absolutely assured. As I believe you know, I have missed no occasion that has offered itself to hold you up as an example of what the best American manhood should stand for. Your fine humanitarian spirit, your unwavering integrity, your magnificent courage have always appealed to me as ideals to which the American people might look for inspiration.

I say all this to indicate that in my opinion it is inconceivable that you should be directly or indirectly responsible for the great wrong that has been done several millions of American citizens of the Jewish faith by the publication of the article, appearing in the *Dearborn Independent* of May 22 under the title, "The International Jew" and which I learn is to be followed by a series of articles of similar purport.[16]

The letter did nothing to change Ford's course. Even Edsel's urging for his father to put an end to the articles did nothing to sway the elder Ford's opinion. Ford felt that the articles did not hurt the "average" Jew but that the "average," hardworking Jew appreciated the supposedly eye-opening series. A September article made the point that

Jewry is not a democracy but an autocracy. Of course the ordinary Jew does not know! The question is, why should he revile the Gentile who tries to tell him? If a Jew will not seal his mind against the statements made in these articles, he will find in his own knowledge sufficient corroboration of their principal features, and he will be in a better position to assist in the solution of the Jewish Question. . . . Is there a fear of permitting the average Jew to read this series? Nothing is more desired by those whose purpose it is to lay foundations for the solution of the Jewish Question in America than that every Jew in the United States should know exactly what is being printed here week by week. The Jew has been deceived by his leaders long enough.[17]

Articles that followed claimed that Jews were responsible for the popularity of jazz, speakeasies, and short skirts; that Jews controlled the world press and the gold standard; that banks, and even Wall Street, were at the mercy of the "learned" Jews. Combined, the Jews were responsible for "a marked deterioration in our literature, amusements, and social conduct . . . a general letting down of standards."[18]

The sudden appearance of the articles was topped only by their sudden disappearance in 1922. Before the articles were discontinued, the *Dearborn Independent* reached a subscription count of over 1,400,000, based not on the growing reputation of the paper but on the fact that dealers selling a Model T were required to sell a subscription to the paper at the same time. Not all dealers felt comfortable with the demand; they instead sent paid subscriptions to people picked out of the phone directory. However, a collection of the articles was soon made available to those requesting copies after they were discontinued in the *Dearborn Independent.* Published in four small volumes: volume 1, *The World's Foremost Problem,* 1920; volume 2, *Jewish Activities in the United States,* 1921; volume 3, *Jewish Influence in American Life,* 1921; and volume 4, *Aspects of Jewish Power in the United States,* 1922, the four volumes together were called *The International Jew.* Translations were made, and the book became a best-seller in Germany, where it later appeared next to copies of *Mein Kampf,* Hitler's book containing his plans for Germany and in which Ford was the only American mentioned.

As Ford-for-President clubs continued to spring up around the country, it became apparent why the assault had come to an abrupt halt, and after Ford's meeting with Coolidge in December 1923, it became clear why the articles suddenly reappeared in the *Dearborn Independent* in the spring of 1924. Ford wanted Muscle Shoals; this meant having the support and trust of the American farmer. However, with the growing popularity of farmers' cooperatives this meant that Ford would have to start his fight for Muscle Shoals by discrediting the benefits these organizations had to offer. To this end, the first piece of this renewed effort was titled "Jewish Exploitation of Farmer Organizations." The article lost no time in picking up where its predecessors had left off. The article's opening paragraph read as follows.

> A band of Jews—bankers, lawyers, money-lenders, and agencies, fruit-packers, professional office managers and bookkeeping experts—is on the back of the American Farmer.
> Working occasionally in the open, usually behind a screen of

well paid Gentile fronts, this organization has developed with such amazing rapidity within the past five years that its operations today extend from the Atlantic to the Pacific and from the interior of Canada to the Mexican border.

If it is allowed to continue for another five years, not a grain grower, not a vegetable producer, not an orchardist, save one class in a limited area, will be able to escape it.

Born in the fertile fortune-seeking brain of a young Jew on the Pacific Coast a little more than five years ago, and nurtured by a Jewish official who had the ear of one of the state governments by which

In reporting the Sapiro trial, the editor for the *Detroit Times* combined actual photographs of the participants with "you are there" cartoons. This provided readers an opportunity to get familiar with the trial and to eventually get an update on the trial in a quick and effective manner. In this cartoon, readers are introduced to Sapiro and his reactions to the *Dearborn Independent* articles. (From *Detroit Times*, Detroit, Michigan, April 2, 1927. Approved by Mark Silverman, Publisher and Editor. Reprinted with permission from The Detroit News.)

he was employed, the idea has turned millions away from the pockets of the men who till the soil, and into the hands of the Jews and their followers.[19]

The "young Jew" referred to in the article was a prominent Chicago attorney named Aaron Sapiro. An orphan, Sapiro had grown up in the slums of Oakland, where he had lived in an orphanage for six years. Described as a Horatio Alger type in newspaper articles to follow, Sapiro graduated from school with honors. He moved to Cincinnati, where he studied to be a rabbi at Hebrew Union College. Eight years later he headed to San Francisco, where he studied law at Hastings Law School, graduating in 1911. He became interested in the economics of farming while doing some legal work for the director of the California Marketing Commission. He especially became interested in farm cooperatives, which he described as "organizations in which the farmers get together to sell their products through a central office."[20] Before long, Sapiro's expertise in this area grew to the point where he was working exclusively for a variety of California co-ops, making eighty thousand dollars a year. He learned the business so well that by 1919 he organized new cooperatives around the state and was the lawyer for fourteen of the largest cooperatives on the West Coast. His salary and his expertise now established, Sapiro decided to go national, incorporating ninety associations in thirty-two states and Canada by 1925. Sapiro's cooperative business reached the point that he eventually had a staff of lawyers in San Francisco, Dallas, Chicago, New York, and Washington, DC.[21]

Subsequent articles in the *Dearborn Independent* claimed that the end of the plot was nowhere in sight. The author spoke of unimpeachable sources that warned that once farmers were organized into national associations, "the men who control these associations will be united in one national association. And the men who control this super-association, this Jew directed holding company for all the farmers of America, will not be the farmers of America."

Referring to himself as an "accident of destiny" whose responsibility it was to stop these allegations against Jews and himself,

An orphan who had studied to become a rabbi, Sapiro made his mark starting in California, where he organized a number of farmers' cooperatives. From there, Sapiro organized farmers' cooperatives all over the nation and Canada. In this cartoon, he was compared to the characters of American author Horatio Alger, who wrote a series of books for boys. Alger's heroes always rose from tattered poverty to riches and respectability. So successful was Sapiro that by the time his lawsuit went to trial, he had attorneys working for him in San Francisco, Dallas, Chicago, New York, and Washington, DC. (From *Detroit Times*, Detroit, Michigan, April 2, 1927. Approved by Mark Silverman, Publisher and Editor. Reprinted with permission from The Detroit News.)

Sapiro filled a one million dollar libel suit against Ford for defamation of character. The case came to trial on March 1927 in Detroit, with Judge Fred S. Raymond presiding. Ford's defense was that he knew nothing about the articles.

Ford's ridiculous claim was upheld by the first witness to take the stand, William Cameron, who for five days unwaveringly continued to assert under cross-examination that he had never "discussed any article on any Jew with Mr. Ford, that he had never sent his master an advance copy of the magazine, and that he had never

This cartoon pictures Sapiro and his attorney, William H. Gallagher, behind the wheel of a fancy limousine running on a set of $1,000,000 tires, with the diminutive Henry Ford in his homely Model T—his *Dearborn Independent* securely on board—staying comfortably ahead of them. The question, Are they libel to run him down? and the answer, Ask me another, are a direct reference to Ford critics, who in the past had tried to "run him down" but had failed. The response also makes a reference to Ford jokes, which had been around since the heyday of the Model T. (From *Detroit Times,* Detroit, Michigan, March 1927. Approved by Mark Silverman, Publisher and Editor. Reprinted with permission from The Detroit News.)

even seen Henry Ford read a copy of it."[22] If true, this meant that "Mr. Ford's Own Page" had been nothing but a fraud and that the entire basis for the paper had been nothing but a lie. Sapiro's attorney decided that the only person that could prove this statement false was Henry Ford. Papers were served. Ford was scheduled to take the stand on Monday, April 1, 1927; however, the night before his scheduled appearance, before Ford could make it to court, he was involved in an automobile accident. Run off Michigan Avenue less than a mile from Fair Lane by an automobile that sideswiped his car, causing him to go down an embankment and strike a tree, Ford managed to climb out of the car and walk home. He reached the Fair Lane guardhouse, where Clara was made aware of what had happened, and an ambulance was called to rush Ford to Henry Ford Hospital. The next day rumors that the accident was staged mingled with rumors that the men in the other car were trying to kill Ford. Regardless of what was the truth, one thing was for certain: the accident had granted Ford a temporary reprieve from having to testify.

Ford sits smugly in between his attorney, James Reed, who was a U.S. senator from Missouri, and Sapiro's attorney, William H. Gallagher. Though this cartoon gives the impression that Ford was in the courtroom, he did not make one single appearance at the trial. (From *Detroit Times,* Detroit, Michigan, March 19, 1927. Approved by Mark Silverman, Publisher and Editor. Reprinted with permission from The Detroit News.)

As it turned out, Ford never did take the stand in the case, because a mistrial was declared on Thursday, April 21, 1927, after one of the jurors, Mrs. Cora Hoffman, who was already under investigation for allegedly accepting a bribe in the case, had given an interview to newspapers. In granting the Ford camp's motion for a mistrial, Judge Raymond said that "in all fairness to the juror in question, it must be stated that up until this time, the investigation did not disclose any facts that warrant the filing of charges against her on a matter that would be very serious if true."[23]

Judge Raymond went on to say that "I have no evidence whatever that Mr. Sapiro, the plaintiff in this case, has indulged himself in any improper conduct in reference to the jury."[24]

Finally, Judge Raymond declared that the trial might have continued "if it had not been for the newspapers, which went so far as to intrude upon the duties of court."[25] Sapiro's attorney argued that Ford's counsel sought a mistrial for the sole purpose of keeping Ford off the stand. "It is our frank belief," said Sapiro's attor-

SOMEHOW WILLIAM J.
CAMERON DID NT LOOK
AT HOME ON THE WITNESS
STAND.

William J. Cameron, editor of the *Dearborn Independent*, admitted under direct examination that the majority of the statements contained in the articles on which the libel suit was based ran without his own knowledge of all the facts. To most of Gallagher's questions, Cameron answered, "I don't know" or "I don't recall." When asked, "Did you discuss with Mr. Ford the publication of any articles dealing with Mr. Sapiro?" Cameron answered, "Not before they were published." Though Cameron lost his position as editor of the *Dearborn Independent* following the trial, he remained a trusted Ford employee for years to come. Since Ford did not appear at the trial, all cartoonists could do was ridicule the other players, as well as Ford's absence. (From *Detroit Times*, Detroit, Michigan, March 1927. Approved by Mark Silverman, Publisher and Editor. Reprinted with permission from The Detroit News.)

ney, William Henry Gallagher, "that this situation clearly discloses that the purpose of the defendant's attorneys is not to obtain justice here, but to procure a postponement of a verdict and to place the case in the unknown future for trial."[26]

The court was adjourned, the jury dismissed. The retrial was scheduled for September 1927.

The case never did go to trial a second time. Tired of the bat-

The Office Secret

Long a voice criticizing the politics and policies of Henry Ford, the *Detroit Saturday Night,* which by this time was led by the original editor of the *Dearborn Independent,* E. G. Pipp, published this cartoon under the headline "When Henry Takes His Pen in Hand." While on the stand, Cameron admitted that he had written the very first article that ran under the heading "Mr. Ford's Own Page." When asked if he had discussed the article's contents with Mr. Ford, Cameron replied, "No; I never had seen Mr. Ford. The ideas I expressed were the ideas Mr. Pipp had given me as those of Mr. Ford." (From *Detroit Saturday Night,* Detroit, Michigan, March 23, 1927.)

tle, Ford took it upon himself to apologize for the articles. On July 8, 1927, Ford issued the following statement, which was published in papers all over the country. It read as follows.

> In the multitude of my activities it has been impossible for me to devote personal attention to their management or to keep informed as to their contents. It has therefore inevitably followed that the con-

A WITNESS STAND
SUGGESTION FOR MR. FORD

Even though Ford used bodyguards to keep away attorneys attempting to serve him with a subpoena to testify, one clever lawyer posed as a reporter at a celebration. When volunteers were sought to clear the room of smokers, the attorney stepped forward. Spying Ford seated inside a Lincoln, the attorney dropped the subpoena and the five-dollar witness fee on Ford's lap. Ray Dahlinger, who had accompanied Ford on the peace ship and was a guest at the party, grabbed the attorney and said, "You think you're pretty smart, don't you? Well, you didn't serve a subpoena on Mr. Henry Ford at all. You served it on Mr. Ford's brother, John Ford." When the incident was reported in court, Reed agreed to have Mr. Ford in the courtroom by the next day. In this cartoon, taken from a collage of cartoons regarding the trial, a clever artist suggested the perfect seat for Mr. Ford to take once on the stand. Note the association with Ford's now outdated Model T. (From *Detroit Times,* Detroit, Michigan, March 1927. Approved by Mark Silverman, Publisher and Editor. Reprinted with permission from The Detroit News.)

duct and policies of these publications had to be delegated to men whom I placed in charge of them and upon whom I relied implicitly.

To my great regret I have learned that Jews generally, and particularly those of this country, not only resent these publications as promoting anti-Semitism, but regard me as their enemy. Trusted friends with whom I have conferred recently have assured me in all sincerity

The verdict of mistrial delivered by Judge Fred S. Raymond yesterday makes Aaron Sapiro, the plaintiff, a victim of circumstances.

Before Ford had a chance to take the stand, Judge Fred S. Raymond declared a mistrial after Mrs. Cora Hoffman, a juror in the trial, granted an interview to reporters. In the interview, Hoffman told reporters that she felt Ford's counsel did not want the case to go to the jury. In granting the mistrial, Judge Raymond said, "After reading the morning paper, it was hardly necessary to listen to the arguments of counsel. It was one of the most flagrant violations of the duty owed this court." Finally, in a comment that sounds reminiscent of highly publicized court cases today, Judge Raymond stated that the trial might have continued "if it had not been for the newspapers, which went so far as to intrude upon the duties of the court" ("Mistrial Verdict Follows Woman Juror's Interview," *Detroit Times*, 21 April 1927). (From *Detroit Times*, Detroit, Michigan, April 1927. Approved by Mark Silverman, Publisher and Editor. Reprinted with permission from The Detroit News.)

SENATOR REED
TAKES THINGS VERY
QUIETLY.

Seen as a steady and unshakable guiding force behind Ford's defense, Reed fell
ill while on a train ride to Detroit from Washington, DC. He was taken to Henry
Ford Hospital with gallbladder problems. He was not in the courtroom on the
day Judge Raymond declared the mistrial. (From *Detroit Times*, Detroit, Michigan,
March 1927. Approved by Mark Silverman, Publisher and Editor. Reprinted with
permission from The Detroit News.)

that in their opinion the character of the charges and insinuations
made against the Jews, both individually and collectively, contained
in many of the articles which have been circulated periodically in the
Dearborn Independent, and have been reprinted in the pamphlets mentioned, justifies the righteous indignation entertained by the Jews
everywhere toward me because of the mental anguish occasioned by
the unprovoked reflections made upon them.

This has led me to direct my personal attention to this subject, in
order to ascertain the exact nature of these articles. As a result of this
survey I confess that I am deeply mortified that this journal, which is
intended to be constructive and not destructive, has been made the
medium for resurrecting exploded fictions, for giving currency to the

WILLIAM H. GALLAGHER
IN ACTION

Cartoonists could not resist portraying Sapiro's representative, William H. Gallagher, as a temperamental attorney, something he was known for up to the end of the trial. Although Gallagher argued that his client was prepared to move forward with an eleven-member jury, Judge Raymond would have nothing to do with it. In the end, Gallagher declared that "no other plaintiff in history faced the obstacles confronting Sapiro." He pointed out that the trial was "held in Ford's hometown" and charged Ford's attorneys with "persistent efforts to delay and drag out the case." (From *Detroit Times,* Detroit, Michigan, March 1927. Approved by Mark Silverman, Publisher and Editor. Reprinted with permission from The Detroit News.)

so-called protocols of the wise men of Zion, which have been demonstrated, as I learn, to be gross forgeries, and for contending that the Jews have been engaged in a conspiracy to control the capital and the industries of the world, besides laying at their door many offenses against decency, public order and good morals.

Had I appreciated even the general nature, to say nothing of the details of these utterances, I would have forbidden their circulation without a moment's hesitation, because I am fully aware of the virtues of the Jewish people as a whole, of what they and their ancestors have done for civilization and for mankind toward the development of commerce and industry, of their sobriety and diligence, their benevolence and their unselfish interest in the public welfare.

OUT OF GA$
No Funds Available for Court Expenses

Even though funds from the Department of Justice fueled the Ford trial for a few days while the department investigated charges of jury tampering by Sapiro, the trial was soon "out of gas" when no evidence was uncovered to substantiate the allegations. (From *Detroit Times*, Detroit, Michigan, April 1927. Approved by Mark Silverman, Publisher and Editor. Reprinted with permission from The Detroit News.)

Of course there are black sheep in every flock, as there are among men of all races, creeds and nationalities who are at times evildoers. It is wrong, however, to judge a people by a few individuals, and I therefore join in condemning unreservedly all wholesale denunciations and attacks.

Those who know me can bear witness that it is not my nature to inflict insult upon and to occasion pain to anybody, and that it has been my effort to free myself from prejudice. Because of that I frankly confess that I have been greatly shocked as a result of my study and examination of the files of the *Dearborn Independent* and of the pamphlets entitled, "*The International Jew*."

I deem it to be my duty as an honorable man to make amends for the wrong done to the Jews as fellow men and brothers, by asking their forgiveness for the harm I have unintentionally committed, by retracting so far as lies within my power the offensive charges laid at their door by these publications, and by giving them unqualified assurance that henceforth they may look to me for friendship and good will.[27]

Response to Ford's statement was swift and pointed. People that agreed with Ford's original sentiments regarding Jews wrote

Admonished by Sapiro in this Polish cartoon, Ford promises never to publish another article attacking Jews in his *Dearborn Independent*. (From *Detroit Polish News*, Detroit, Michigan, July 9, 1927.)

him letters telling him that he had "turned yellow," "was built on the jelly-fish order," "was a pitiful quitter." They charged that he had "sold [his] birthright for a mess of porridge."[28]

The Jewish community's reaction was a bit more positive. In an interview with the *Detroit Times,* Rabbi Franklin urged fellow Jews to forgive Ford by stating that

> Mr. Ford's repudiation in today's papers of the articles attacking Jews in his paper and his appeal for the forgiveness of the Jews as fellow-men and brothers, fully justifies that faith that I expressed in him in a letter written May, 1920, when the first article appeared. I want to be among the very first to have the privilege of congratulating him upon the fine courageous stand he has today taken—a stand that I feel sure will do him honor not only at the hands of the Jews of the world, but of all brothermen of every faith and every creed. I trust that it may be my privilege to resume with Mr. Ford those fine, friendly relations which through so many years it was mine to enjoy.
>
> Despite the continuance of these articles in *The Dearborn Independent,* I have felt all along that Mr. Ford had not sensed their inherent injustice to uncounted thousands of Jewish people the world over and I could not believe that a man of Mr. Ford's native humanitarian instincts would sanction a course that could create nothing but hate and injustice and suffering.[29]

Julius Rosenwald, a Chicago philanthropist, echoed Rabbi Franklin's sentiments in saying that

> Mr. Ford's statement is very greatly belated. This letter would have been very much greater to his credit had it been written five years ago. It seems almost impossible to believe he has not been deluged with evidence on the very facts which he now seems to realize are true.
>
> But it is never too late to make amends, and I congratulate Mr. Ford that he has at last seen the light. He will find that the spirit of forgiveness is not entirely a Christian virtue, but is equally a Jewish virtue.[30]

The day after Ford's apology, according to the *New York Times,* the *Dearborn Independent* made "no reference to the anti-Jewish campaign and 'Mr. Ford's Own Page' [was] devoted to a discussion

With the close of the Sapiro trial, Ford and the rest of the country now prepared themselves for the unveiling of the Model A, the car that would supplant the Tin Lizzie. With Ford automobile sales slumping, Ford finally agreed to the change after years of prodding from his son, Edsel, as well as from a number of Ford executives. Cartoons depicting the anticipated birth of a new Ford became as plentiful as Model T cartoons and the Ford jokes of the past. (From *Post-Gazette*, Pittsburgh, Pennsylvania, December 2, 1927. Copyright, Graphic Reprint/*Pittsburgh Post-Gazette*, 2000 all rights reserved. Reprinted with permission.)

of 'the limitation of education.' "[31] It was as if the entire series of events had never taken place.

Final word was left to Sapiro, who said, "The retraction, apology and recantation have fulfilled the purpose of the suit, so far as the main intention is concerned. I certainly have no desire to cause Mr. Ford any embarrassment whatsoever and I mean that to apply from all standpoints."[32]

The suit was settled out of court. Ford promised not to print offensive articles in the future and to take the *International Jew* off the market. Liebold was relieved from his duties as general manager of the paper. Cameron was also dismissed, although both men stayed in the employ of Ford Motor Company. Subscriptions to the *Dearborn Independent* were no longer accepted. Ford stated that he would make the paper an in-house publication. However, by December 1927, the paper folded completely.

The year 1923 had found Ford on the verge of the presidency, acquiring Muscle Shoals seemed like a real possibility, his opinions found a voice in the *Dearborn Independent,* and his ghostwritten autobiography was a best-seller. It had seemed as if there was nothing Henry Ford could not do—and now, only four years later, it had all come crashing down.

Ford, and the nation's newspapers, however, did not spend too much time thinking about the present. They were too busy getting ready for the unveiling of the Model A—the car that was destined to replace the never changing, always dependable Model T. It seemed that Ford was not the only one ready to turn over a new leaf.

CHAPTER 8

A Case of "Ford-osis":
The Hatching of the Model A

"I WILL BUILD A MOTOR CAR for the great multitude," Ford had proudly announced prior to the debut of the Model T in 1908. By 1927, 15,500,000 Model Ts had been sold in America. An additional 1,000,000 were sold in Canada, and in Britain the count had reached a quarter of a million. When these numbers were added together, the Model T accounted for 50 percent of the automobiles sold throughout the world. The Model T had indeed fulfilled Ford's vision and mission; the Model T was the "universal car," the car that put the world on wheels.

So sure was Ford concerning his vision for the Model T that in 1909, he told his stockholders that the Model T would be the only car manufactured by Ford Motor Company. By this time Ford owned 58 percent of the company; there was little anyone could do to stop him. Although the Dodge brothers finally succeeded in slowing him down with their court action in 1916, they were in no position to argue their case at that time. Not only was the Model T not taken out of production, it remained virtually unchanged for the next fifteen years and rightfully so, outselling every car in the world from one year to the next.

However, by 1924, America's love affair with the Model T began to cool. Dealers complained about the car's planetary transmission, its lack of a self-starter, the absence of a gas gauge on the dash, and the awkward position of the spare tire, which was bolted under the car. It was time for a body with style and engine improvements. Ford responded to dealer demands by saying, "So far as I can see the only trouble with the Ford car is that we can't make them fast enough." Ford seemed to be correct in his assessment of the situation. After all, in the year 1923, 1,699,984 Model T's were sold, as compared to 798,555 cars for General Motors. However, in

This 1914 cartoon featuring the "universal Ford" symbol radiating above the earth praised the number of Model Ts sold by the Booker Auto Company of Grand Rapids, Michigan. The prophetic image of the Model T encircling the earth became a reality in the years to follow, as seen in the fact that it is estimated that from 1917 to 1927 half of the automobiles on the world's roads were Fords. (From *Grand Rapids Herald*, Grand Rapids, Michigan, February 22, 1914.)

1924, the trend started to change, Ford sales went down 15 percent. Ford executives blamed it on a national recession. In 1925, a year of prosperity, General Motors moved ahead, while the Model T fell further behind. Finally, Ford gave in, allowing the Model T's chassis to be lowered. Sales increased but fell off by the end of the year. In 1926, Ford did what he always did when his Model T lagged in sales; he lowered the price—and for the first time this move did nothing to create a demand.[1]

Late in 1926, Edsel persuaded his father to make additional changes to the Model T. After a series of discussions, these changes meant that

> the car's fenders were cupped, its windshield slanted, its body lengthened and lowered, its radiator rounded off, its gas tank placed under the hood . . . , even its black color was discarded. The late 1926

Model T could be had in fawn gray, gun-metal blue, phoenix brown, and highland green. The result: Ford production dropped by more than a quarter of a million while General Motors' sales came within a few thousand of Ford. Chevrolet sold more than 600,000 cars. Henry was warned by a writer in *Automotive Industry* that "The American public was still buying about twice as many Fords as Chevrolets, but it had bought about six times as many as recently as 1924. And, comparisons aside, Ford's own production record showed a decline of more than 300,000 cars in the past twelve months."[2]

By 1926 Chevrolet, Dodge, and a handful of other carmakers had slashed their prices significantly, cutting into Model T sales. At the same time Oldsmobile and Essex introduced an affordable V-6 engine. These new cars equaled the Tin Lizzie in price while incorporating several innovations and style features that the public now desired in their cars.

As pointed out by David L. Lewis in his book *The Public Image of Henry Ford*, the first significant clue that a change was in the works appeared when a dealer for Ford Motor Company turned down a large order of Model Ts from the Detroit Police Department early in 1927.

The company, when asked about the refused order, said they were not discontinuing the Model T. However, on May 25 a wire went out to dealers across the country from Edsel Ford announcing that the Model T would go out of production and a new model would be taking its place later in the year. The next day the fifteen millionth Model T rolled out of Highland Park, and the announcement that Model T production would cease was made to the public. This milestone marked the final days of one of the most successful production runs of any model of car in the world.

Production of the Model T at Highland Park was brought to a halt in the summer of 1927. Sixty thousand Detroiters found themselves out of work. The move surprised economists the world over. The year was an economic boom; why would Ford make a decision to change everything now? The *New York World* estimated that five hundred thousand workers from a variety of industries would be affected in one way or another.[3]

Ford supplied absolutely no details on the new model with the

Though Ford had promised a "complete description" of the new model "within a few weeks" after the initial May 25 new-car announcement nothing followed until August 10. Critics claimed that no news was bad news. Rumors that Ford was having problems with the design, equipment, and manufacture of the Model A led critics to believe and report that the car to be unveiled on December 2, 1927, was the best the company could do at the time. In this cartoon, a diapered Model A screams out for another $1,000,000 in research and development, while a concerned Henry and an anxious "Detroit" grandmother work to calm the newborn baby. (From *Dayton Daily News,* Dayton, Ohio, December 1, 1927. Copyright, Graphic Reprint/*Dayton Daily News,* all rights reserved.)

On August 10, 1927, Edsel Ford announced that "the new Ford automobile is an accomplished fact. The engineering problems affecting its design and equipment and affecting also its manufacture have all been solved. . . . The tests already made show it is faster, smoother, more rugged and more flexible than we had hoped for in the early stages of designing" (quoted in David L. Lewis, *The Public Image of Henry Ford*). This was to be the last Ford Motor Company statement issued until October 11. While the "motoring public" waited, wondering what to name the new car, scores of photographers descended on Highland Park hoping to get footage of the new vehicle. Scores of cartoons speculating on the name and looks of the car added to the anticipation generated by Ford's secrecy. (From *Dallas Morning News*, Dallas, Texas, December 1927. Reprinted with permission of The Dallas Morning News.)

announcement, mostly because at the time there were no details available. The new model was still in the planning stages. The ensuing months saw a flood of widespread and often hilarious speculation as to what the new Ford would look like. A whimsical belief that Mr. Ford might work yet another miracle was in the air. How could a new Ford car be anything less than what the Model T had been to so many people in its own time? Ideas ranged from the practical inclusion of a standard transmission to the futuristic

WHEN RUMOR GETS THROUGH WITH IT

In anticipation of the Model A's coming out party, the following poem, which gave birth to the cartoon shown here, ran in the *Great Divide* of Denaw, Colorado. The poem, titled "The New Ford," read "The new Ford car, Dame Rumor says, / Will have a Turkish bath attached; / A radio that sweetly plays the moment that the door's unlatched; / An ice machine, a baby grand, a year's supply of pepsin gum, / an earth-indicator compass and a sun-porch, or solarium. / (P.S.—I have to mention, tho, that Edsel says it isn't so.)" (From *New York World,* New York, December 1927.)

addition of statues on the running board and precious stones as rivets holding the car together. This rampant speculation also demonstrated that people were not willing to let the old faithful Model T be replaced by just another ordinary car.

Following the announcement, interest surrounding the Model A grew with each passing day. Newspapers, however, did not tell their readership that Ford's competitors were already changing over from one model to the next without a break in production; they completely ignored the fact that Ford could not promise to deliver a car to dealers on time, even after the car was offered to the public; they wrote nothing about a competitor's car being lower priced; and they did not mention that Ford's automotive improvements had been available in a competitor's model years before. As Ralph Z. Thatcher points out in an article for the *Detroit News*,

> Judging from the cry that went up about this new car, you would think that Ford had accomplished something revolutionary when he equipped it with a standard gear shift, brakes all around, and other appendages. Seems to me that all these things already were a part of other automobiles costing not much more than Fords, and that all Ford did was to make his car conventional.[4]

Images of Ford at work on the new model appeared in the papers throughout the summer and well into the winter months. Ford appeared in simple work clothes, such as he might have worn in the old days when he first started in the automotive industry. It was Ford himself who was shown tinkering with the chassis or tweaking the engine as the world waited eagerly, peeking over his shoulder. Ford personally directed much of the research that went into the Model A, but the image of Ford in back of his house tinkering in the garage was what the public envisioned since he was the people's industrialist, the man who had brought the car to the common folk. In other, less flattering cartoons Ford is characterized as a fat chicken sitting on an egg or looking over a nest awaiting the arrival of the car. Whether Ford appeared as a country bumpkin or a mother hen, these images recalled his rural past and populist ethics.

On October 11, 1927, Edsel Ford announced that the Model A would start rolling off the assembly line within a few days. He also reported to the press that 125,000 units had been ordered by dealers. In response to the number of units ordered, the *Lynn Telegram-News* from Massachusetts said that this was "a demonstration of faith and confidence in Ford which has no precedent in world history." (From *Des Moines Register*, Des Moines, Iowa, September 30, 1927. Copyright, Graphic Reprint/*Des Moines Dispatch*, all rights reserved.)

Before production could start on the Model A forty thousand machines capable of manufacturing nothing but a Model T were removed from the Rouge complex. In addition, thirty-four domestic assembly plants, twelve overseas plants, and countless supply shops had to be overhauled before a single Model A could be produced. The first Model A was completed on October 21, 1927, and by November 1, twenty cars a day, on the average, were being manufactured. The birds in the cartoon shown here—with the exception of the "Pioneer Model T"—represented the various features that Henry could choose from in putting together his Model A. Just exactly what the new car would look like once it was hatched was anybody's guess. It is interesting to point out that even with the passage of time, cartoonists still made reference to Henry's utilitarian background when it fit their needs. (From *Montgomery Adventure,* Montgomery, Alabama, November 26, 1927.)

On November 25, 1927, Edsel Ford announced that the Model A would make its debut on December 2. Knowing that the Model A was on the way, car buyers waited until its appearance before making a new car purchase. This caused a decline of one million in the number of passenger cars sold in 1927 as compared to 1926. For those that owned a Model T, farewells would certainly be a heart-wrenching experience; after all, the dependable Model T had always been there for them. As suggested by the cartoon shown here, the Model T was more than a car; it was a living, breathing "'ol' gal" complete with a soul. (From *New York World*, November 1927.)

At the same time that the excitement about the new model mounted, a nostalgia for the old Tin Lizzie took shape. Epitaphs were written, and fond memories were exchanged concerning the outdated Model T. People declared it the greatest invention of the age over and above the telephone, the telegraph, and many other inventions of the time. The rattling body and homely looks suddenly became honored aspects of its simplistic beauty. America found it hard to let go of the little car that had chugged and rattled the population into the twentieth century. Overnight it became an icon for bygone days of innocent fun and freedom.

Ford jokes reappeared in the nostalgic atmosphere with sentimental overtones. The old jokes about the Model T's homely looks or rattling ride reappeared as the Model T was compared to the possibilities of the new model.

Lizzie appeared in many cartoons as the older noisy sibling or the forgotten wife abandoned at home. The Model A was the fresh

The Girl He Left Behind

The steam from the Model T's radiator hisses, "Forsaken am I," as Ford drives away in his new sweetheart, "Elsie." Ford, dressed in his "Sunday-go-to-meeting" outfit, smiles with satisfaction—probably at the suggested acceleration of the car. While the Model A ended up looking nothing like this cartoonist's rendition, it is safe to say that Ford never lost the smile pictured on his face, especially after the car's success. (From *Detroit Times,* Detroit, Michigan, December 10, 1927. Approved by Mark Silverman, Publisher and Editor. Reprinted with permission from The Detroit News.)

newborn babe or the tantalizing mistress. Each of these cartoons tapped into a feeling Americans had that they were somehow abandoning an old friend by leaving the Model T behind, even though it had been several years since many of these same people had actually owned one of the Tin Lizzies. All the same, the image of Ford remained true to conclusions that had been drawn at the start of his appearance in editorial and political cartoons—it was Henry Ford against the world! It was "good 'ol Henry Ford" facing yet another challenge. Could he succeed? Would his Model A be better than or even equal to the Model T? Would Henry Ford come through for the nation's economy? Would he come through for the common person yet again? Was there anything that could keep Henry Ford down?

By not releasing any details on the Model A from the outset, Ford stumbled upon a free publicity campaign like no other in advertising history. The lack of information created a vast market for speculation in every major newspaper in the country. As the summer of 1927 waned and excitement mounted, more and more stories about the possible design of the new Ford appeared in papers and conversations all around the country and even around the world. Some businesspeople felt that the lack of information was a vulpine move on Ford's part to save a buck on advertising and create excitement. It is more likely that lack of any details was the root of the "no information" policy at first. When Ford actually settled on the specifics of the car, he took advantage of the situation and created more hysteria deliberately.

During the fall of 1927, prospective car buyers held out on purchasing a car until the release of the Model A. Several businesspeople, including bankers and newspaper editors, later attributed a slight recession to the drop in car sales. They felt that the reinstatement of full production at the Ford plant, which had been suspended since the end of May, would lift the economy out of the recession.

When the Model A finally arrived on the market on December 2, 1927, crowds flocked to the dealerships to get a glimpse of the new Ford. One hundred thousand people packed Detroit showrooms.[5] Police in Cleveland were called to control the crowds. In New York, the dealer finally rented Madison Square Gardens for a

THE NEW FORD CAR TO THE RESCUE

When the Model A was introduced, more than 400,000 orders went on the company books in less than fourteen days. By January 10, 1928, 727,000 were sold. The car was a critical and popular success. Sales of the Model A surpassed all expectations, aiding the economy of the world along the way. Ford and his automobile had come to the rescue once again as seen in this 1927 drawing. (From *Chicago Daily Tribune,* Chicago, Illinois, December 3, 1927. Copyrighted Chicago Tribune Company. All rights reserved. Used with permission.)

week to accommodate the throngs of people who came to view the Model A. By the end of that week over 1,250,000 New Yorkers saw the Model A. David L. Lewis states that

> in towns where no Fords were placed on display, the populace saw movies of the car or gawked at photographs. More than ten million persons, 8.5 percent of the nation's population, saw the actual car within the first thirty-six hours of its showing. Within less than a week, more than twenty-five million Americans had seen the new vehicle. Overseas, special trains were run to London for thousands eager to view the car; Berlin police had to fight back the throngs outside the

LIZZIE'S GOT A LITTLE SISTER

A couple of days after the Model A's unveiling, the *New York World* wrote that the Model A had exceeded all expectations. "Even the most godless scoffer," the paper reported, "must have realized that the magnum opus thus offered for sale was worth all the commotion it was causing." Most important of all, however, was the fact that people seeing the car had pronounced "Lizzie's" little sister a success. Ford, through no effort on his part, was praised for his innovative genius. He was given full credit for the new Model A, even though a number of individuals, including Edsel Ford, had contributed to its completed form. In this cartoon, the proud parent, Henry Ford, carries out his newborn baby from the Ford factory. "The Public" stands watching from a distance, not sure if the time is right to approach. If the screaming baby is any indication, the birth must not have been an easy one. (From *New York World*, New York, December 2, 1927.)

exhibition rooms; and 150,000 Spaniards attended the Madrid showing. Never in the world's history had a vehicle aroused such excitement.[6]

The *New York World* reported that "even the most godless scoffer must have realized that the magnum opus thus offered for sale was worth all the commotion it was causing." The *New York*

Times wrote that "if stroked gently he [meaning Ford dealers] would purr." Even Ford's advertising strategy was praised with such comments as "the most amazing publicity coup of modern times"; "the greatest publicity stunt of all times"; "the greatest showman in American business." "Had the talents of the late P. T. Barnum, the brothers Ringling, and Tes Rickard been united in one grand effort," wrote one commentator, "it is doubtful whether they could have brought to pass any such spectacle as that of Friday, December 2."[7]

While the Model A proved much more conventional than many had speculated, it was a superior car for its time. It was quiet and offered a smooth ride. The new Ford included safety glass, the newer balloon tires, and a standard stick shift transmission. The latest in shock absorption and padding was included for a smoother ride, and the design was rounded and more in keeping with the styles of the day. The new additions did not jack up the sticker price. Most of these new cars came in at under five hundred dollars. By January 10, 1928, 727,000 cars were sold. The Model A was considered stylish yet affordable, and many famous Americans ordered one immediately, giving the car much more prestige than its predecessor. Sales in 1929 reached 1,851,092, which represented 34 percent of the market share. According to David L. Lewis, "In 1930 Ford's car outsold the entire line of General Motors by about 300,000 units. During 1929 and 1930 Ford's profits (after taxes) exceeded $131,000,000, a sum which more than offset the $101,000,000 lost during 1927 and 1928."[8]

All in all, Ford, through silence and perfectly timed announcements, had pulled off one of his greatest coups. The public response to Ford was a symptom of a societal disease that Ralph Z. Thatcher believed had been growing since Ford's introduction of the five-dollar day. He called the disorder "Ford-osis." In his tongue-in-cheek article titled "Have You a Case of Ford-osis, Too?" Thatcher wrote

> Ford-osis, it's on the brain and in the blood of the American people. They gobble the Ford stuff, and never stop to reason whether they like it, or whether it has any real merit in it. They don't measure Henry by the same yardstick they apply to the rest of humankind.

THE NEW MODEL

By New Year's Day, 1928, Ford Motor Company had produced a mere 125 to 140 cars—nowhere near enough to fulfill demand. However, by midyear production numbers had reached 4,000, and by the end of the year the number grew to 800,000. Meanwhile, Chevrolet manufactured and sold over 1,000,000 cars in 1928 to maintain its number one ranking in automotive sales. This supremacy would come crashing down in 1929 when the Model A outsold the Chevrolet by 34 percent. As suggested by this cartoon, the world had indeed taken on a new shape influenced by the new Ford car. (From *New York World*, New York, December 2, 1928.)

> Some of his words and acts, if spoken and done by any other man, would strike you as being more or less silly. Yet, under the spell of Ford-osis, you would hail them as matters of boundless consequence, and you would be the first to snatch from the fingers of a screaming newsboy the edition that breaks the news to the world.[9]

Business was not to remain this successful for long, not with the Great Depression looming on the horizon and the competition hot on Ford's heels. By 1931, Ford realized that his Model A was not going to satisfy the public for long. The Model A was no Model T. Ford, ready for his next challenge, shut down production of the Model A on August 1931.

History, however, shows that Ford's Model A, at least during its first year of existence, was everything that the public wanted and demanded that Henry Ford deliver. In the end, Ford and his car overcame all obstacles once again—the man and his automobile were infallible in the public's mind, and the public was sure that whatever Henry Ford decided to embark upon in the future, it was sure to change the world.

CHAPTER 9

Ford, Newspapers, and Cartoons: From Obscurity to Legend

AFTER READING THE TEXT and viewing the many cartoons found in this volume, the reader may ask if Ford was aware of his portrayal in newspapers and cartoons. To this question there is no clear answer. Ford never did release a public statement specifically addressing this subject. What history does show, however, is that Ford was a great fan of news that concerned him, his family, or Ford Motor Company. This claim can be substantiated in a number of ways, starting with the fact that Ford employed several newspaper clipping services charged with sending him all published materials concerning the Fords, which included cartoons. From servants that worked for Henry and Clara Ford at Fair Lane, we learn that in their private lives Henry and Clara enjoyed listening to radio broadcasts about themselves, as well as recorded interviews of themselves. Furthermore, we know Ford followed newspaper accounts of his life, because he often chastised his Fair Lane houseman, John Williams, for moving newspaper clippings from the spot where Ford remembered leaving them. On one occasion, Williams recalled, Ford was so upset with him for moving his newspaper clippings that he did not calm down until he found out that they had been moved at Clara's request.[1]

What did Ford think about cartoons that praised and lambasted the popular scene in general? Again, Ford is silent on the subject; however, we do know that the magazine *Ford Times* often carried humorous cartoons poking fun at the Model T and that the magazine published cartoons that ridiculed the rich for not buying a Model T. We also know that Ford printed humorous and editorial cartoons in his *Dearborn Independent* and that cartoons often graced the front page of Ford's newspaper. From this evidence, we can, at the very least, ascertain that Ford knew that the public expected cartoons in their newspapers and magazines.

Perhaps the most intriguing question of all has to be, what did Ford think of cartoons that took aim at him? To this question, there is an answer. The answer does not come through the words of Henry Ford but through his actions, as evidenced in the following account found in David E. Nye's book *Henry Ford, Ignorant Idealist.*

> Ford's favorite cartoon came from the period when he closed his factory. In the drawing, Ford stands in the middle of a narrow road surrounded by automobile parts which prevent other motorists, representing his competitors, from passing him. Ford liked this cartoon so much he had it framed and hung in his office.[2]

This cartoon, which is titled, "Henry's New Model," is included in chapter 8. It was published by the *Des Moines Register* on September 30, 1927. This cartoon was also the only one of its kind reproduced in *The Ford Road,* the official Ford Motor Company book celebrating the company's seventy-fifth anniversary.[3] The cartoon not only shows all of the images mentioned previously, it also shows Ford holding the thumb on his left hand to his nose and wagging his fingers at those waiting impatiently around him. It is almost as if the gesture represents what Ford thought about the critics and doubters that hounded his every decision up to that point in his career.

Regardless of what Ford thought about cartoons depicting his life and career, the fact remains that his life played itself out perfectly for the cartoonists and newspaper reporters. In fact, Fred Black, a close associate of Ford, summed it up best when he wrote in his personal reminiscences that

> any Ford legend would start with the boss himself, and it was nursed along by the newspapermen, rather than engineered by any staff at Ford's. . . . actually, Henry Ford was the top guy as far as creating situations that resulted in some of the top stories. . . . Nobody made Henry Ford from a publicity standpoint except himself.[4]

Of course, the world would never have been introduced to the caricature of Henry Ford if he had not achieved success with his Model T. After all, consumers first fell in love with the price of the Model T, and then they fell in love with the car and all that it represented. They could not help themselves. Here was an automobile that was made especially for them. It was not a gas-guzzler that was prized by the wealthy; it was a means by which everyday people gained their freedom. Yet it was so much more than that. The Model T worked the farm, cut timber, and drove over deep rutted roads. It was dependable. You could trust a Ford, because a Ford would never let you down. Soon the Model T became a member of the family, a family member that critics often placed in the role of the humble stepsister or the skinny kid who gets sand kicked in his face by the muscle-bound bully. In order to protect this valued family member, those that owned it started to make up jokes and draw cartoons to make themselves and the Model T feel better. For example, there was no better sight in the world than a rich man stopping to buy gas for his oversized gas-guzzler as the Model T kept rolling down the road. For the owners of the Model T owning the car gave them permission to brag about their common sense, their individuality, and their ability to get through any rut-infested road in the country. By telling jokes and drawing funny cartoons about the Model T, owners felt better about themselves and their choice to buy and to be seen in a Model T. Soon there was not one bad thing someone could say about a Model T that the owner could not deflect with a joke or by referencing a cartoon in the *Ford Times,* in a Ford joke book, or in the newspapers.

After establishing the Model T in the eyes of the common people, Ford worked hard to convince the rich to give the Model T a chance. He did this by publicizing the fact that movie stars, presidents, and heads of state could be spotted cruising around in the Model T. When this campaign was combined with the Model T's debut on America's silver screen, in which the car costarred with the Keystone Kops and Laurel and Hardy, the Model T was accepted by everyone, including the rich. For one thing, the audience could now argue that the Model T had no stand-in, because what the audience was seeing on the movie screen was something an owner of a Model T had already tried or was going to try with the Model T.

Before long the Model T was much more than a car, and the name Model T was not enough to capture the car's persona. Therefore the nickname "Tin Lizzie" was born and can today be found in *Merriam Webster's Collegiate Dictionary,* tenth edition, with the following information on its origin: "nickname for the Model T Ford automobile." The definition provided is "a small inexpensive early automobile." The name stuck, and soon songs, poems, and even a symphony were written about the Tin Lizzie. Sure, the Model T was sometimes stubborn and at times fought back by breaking an arm or a jaw as its owner tried to start it up using the hand crank, but if an owner took care of the Model T, it was loyal to the very end—so loyal in fact that some argued that it challenged the dog for the title of man's best friend. All in all it took Ford roughly eight years to firmly establish the legend of the Model T. Once this was done and his financial base was secure, Ford was now ready to step out of the limelight created by his Model T.

Henry Ford was not the only man who had grown rich and had established a public image for himself thanks to the automobile. In Michigan alone, Ransom E. Olds and the Dodge brothers had become so wealthy that their pockets were lined with millions. However, while they were spending their money building lavish homes and acquiring real estate throughout the world, Henry Ford decided to give away ten million dollars to his employees. Again, some would argue as to who came up with the idea of the five-dollar day. In the end, however, all that mattered was that Henry Ford took full advantage of the publicity generated by his decision to make his workforce the highest paid in the world. Ford was no longer just the name of a car; it was the name of a real man—the man that had dreamed up and built the Model T. After the five-dollar-a-day announcement the country found out that the Model T was a lot like Henry Ford. The image presented of Ford was that he was from a farm, worked hard, and was dependable and giving. He was trustworthy. He did not build elaborate mansions with his money. He gave it away. But most important, Henry did not have to step on anybody's back to make it to the top; he had made it through hard work and honesty. Certainly Ford changed his mind, and certainly he sometimes had a hard time making up his mind or getting started, but when he did there was no stopping him! If Ford was on the job things were going to get done, like it or not.

When newspaper reporters covering the announcement of the five-dollar day arrived in Detroit on January 6, 1914, they found themselves no more knowledgeable than the general public; they knew nothing about Henry Ford the man. Some reporters flatly stated that when they first came to Michigan there was no established Ford legend because success had come too quickly for Ford. For this reason, reporters first had to learn who Ford was and from where he had come. More than that, reporters had to establish the Ford legend in the minds of the general public. They did this by interviewing Henry Ford; thus the Ford legend came straight from the mouth of Henry Ford. Newspapers also had to show the public what Henry Ford looked like. This was accomplished by publishing penciled drawings side by side with the biographies of Ford. From these stories people came to know and recognize Ford as a farm boy made good. The public also realized that the Model T contained many of the characteristics found in Henry Ford's background and personality.

Meanwhile, cartoonists focused on the effect the five-dollar-a-day announcement had on the common person. They did this because readers did not yet know Henry Ford well enough to understand the implied meaning behind a cartoon. On a more simplistic level, cartoonists did not focus on Henry Ford because they themselves did not even know what Ford looked like. It was not until they saw the penciled portraits and read Ford biographies in the newspapers that they, along with the rest of the country, started to learn what Ford looked like and what his background was. All of these things are important to cartoonists because if no one knows anything about a person or a situation, then no one is going to comprehend the message a cartoonist is trying to communicate. For example, if a young woman is seated on Bill Clinton's lap and he is dressed in a Santa Claus suit and asks her, with a smile on his face, "What do you want for Christmas, young lady?" chances are pretty good that all of us are going to understand the underlying implications of this cartoon. Some of us will laugh; some of us will get angry; but all of us will have an opinion on what the cartoonist is saying. Ford's announcement of the five-dollar day established him in the public eye, and in the interviews that followed, the Ford legend became firmly entrenched.

After the news of the five-dollar day died out, people knew something about Henry Ford. They might not have all the facts, but they knew enough to understand the subtle codes that cartoonists began incorporating into their work.

The following year, 1915, when Ford topped the news of his five-dollar day by announcing that he was going to bring an end to World War I by Christmas, cartoonists knew what Ford looked like and found a wealth of satirical images to pair up with Ford caricatures as part of a lengthy fascination with the story. People recognized Henry Ford in his signature suit and overcoat. They recognized his lean physique and his face. They even knew Ford's background well enough that they understood the references to the farm, as well as to Henry's "can-do" personality. Of course, the public also recognized the absurdity of the moment, which made it perfect material for a comparison to the early jokes that had surrounded the Model T. Cartoonists must have smiled for the entire year, knowing that their employment was guaranteed at least for a while. When the squirrel mascot; Mars, the Roman god of war; and the often scared and beaten angel of peace were thrown into the mix, enough publicity was generated on the subject that readers who previously were not aware of Henry Ford certainly were now.

Once Ford's peace ship initiative failed he felt that people would ridicule him back home, but while some did, most praised Ford for his efforts. While most public careers would have been over at this point, Ford, like his automobile, kept rolling along. Not only did he overcome the embarrassment of the peace ship fiasco, including what some felt was manipulation at the hands of Rosika Schwimmer, he went on to add to his lore: he would have won a seat in the Senate if he had wanted one, and he would have become the president of the United States if he had wished to do so. Through all this, and for the rest of his career, cartoonists never forgot the Ford that was established in 1914 and 1915. Maybe his face grew older, but he never lost his lean and youthful appearance or his do or die attitude that had added to his fame. Perhaps Ford had penciled a caricature of himself long ago—and if not, he had certainly drawn the conclusion that no one could stop Henry Ford but Henry Ford himself.

Notes

CHAPTER 1

1. David L. Lewis, *The Public Image of Henry Ford* (Detroit: Wayne State University Press, 1976), 43.

2. Joseph R. Szczesny, "Cars That Mattered," *Time,* 7 December 1998, 80.

3. Ibid.

4. Robert Lacey, *Ford: The Men and the Machine* (New York: Ballantine Books, 1987), 306.

CHAPTER 2

1. *Everybody's Magazine,* 1 April 1914, p. 465; quoted in Allan Nevins and Frank E. Hill, *Ford: The Times, the Man, the Company* (New York: Charles Scribner's Sons, 1954), 579.

2. Nevins and Hill, *Ford: The Times, The Man, The Company,* 578.

3. Lewis, *Public Image of Henry Ford,* 74.

4. "Henry Ford," advertisement, *New York Times,* 9 January 1914, p. 8.

5. Dixon Wector, *The Hero in America* (Ann Arbor: University of Michigan Press, 1966), 419.

6. Robert Conot, *American Odyssey* (New York: Bantam Books, 1974), 225.

7. Ford received credit for the five-dollar day, although John R. Lee, John Dodge, and the Reverend Samuel Marquis, who succeeded Lee as head of the Ford Motor Company Sociological Department, claim that the idea originated with Sorensen. In his collection of memoirs entitled "Reminiscences," which is housed at the Research Library at the Henry Ford Museum and Greenfield Village, Sorensen states that Ford, Pete Martin, John Lee, and himself were there. Ford had called the meeting determined to institute the five-dollar day. Martin and Lee were against it but gave in; Couzens's mind was changed later after a private conversation with Ford. Even before the two board meetings referred to here, Ford had asked Couzens to prepare financial documents to present to the board. Couzens prepared the information without knowing its purpose.

8. James Couzens, "Minutes of Meeting of the Board of Directors Ford Motor Company" (unpublished, Ford Motor Company Board of Directors Meeting, 5 January 1914).

9. Ibid.

10. "Henry Ford Gives $10,000,000 in 1914 Profits to His Employes [*sic*]," *Detroit Journal,* 5 January 1914, p. 1.

11. Lewis, *Public Image of Henry Ford,* 71.

12. "Sermon Inspired by Ford Bequest," *Detroit News-Tribune,* 12 January 1914, p. 4.

13. "Ford Gift Praised in Many Sermons," *Detroit News,* 12 January 1914, p. 5.

14. "Joy Reigns Supreme among Ford Employees," *Detroit Times,* 12 January 1914, p. 1.

15. The International Harvester Company was located in Chicago. Its size and production numbers equaled those of Ford Motor Company.

16. "Comfortable Homes of Ford Men Sharp Contrast to Hovel of I.H.C. Workers," *Detroit Times,* 16 April 1914, p. 1.

17. "Gives $10,000,000 to 26,000 Employes [*sic*]," *New York Times,* 6 January 1914, p. 1.

18. Carol Gelderman, *Henry Ford: The Wayward Capitalist* (New York: Dial Press, 1981), 53.

19. "Automobile Makers Unable to Follow Ford," *Rochester Union,* 9 January 1914, p. 1.

20. "Press Opinions of the Ford Plan," *Detroit Free Press,* 9 January 1914, p. 3.

21. "Ford's Scheme Is Opposed in London as 'Sensational,' " *Detroit Free Press,* 18 January 1914, p. 1.

22. Quoted in "Press Opinions of the Ford Plan," *Detroit Free Press,* 9 January 1914, p. 3.

23. Lewis, *Public Image of Henry Ford,* 74.

24. "Henry Ford, Who Made 26,000 Employees Happy," *New York Sun,* 11 January 1914, p. 5.

25. Ibid.

26. Ibid.

27. Ibid.

28. "Gold Rush on at Ford Plant: Mob for Jobs," *Detroit Free Press,* 7 January 1914, p. 1.

29. Ibid.

30. "Closed Gates Repulse Ford Gold Seekers," *Detroit Free Press,* 9 January 1914, p. 3.

31. Ibid.

32. "Icy Fire-Hose Deluge Stops 1,200 in Riotous Rush for Ford's Jobs," *Detroit Journal,* 12 January 1914, p. 1.

33. Gelderman, *Henry Ford: The Wayward Capitalist,* 55.

34. Nevins and Hill, *Ford: The Times, the Man, the Company,* 645.

CHAPTER 3

1. Theodore Delavigne, "Henry Ford to Push World-Wide Campaign for Universal Peace: Will Devote Life and Fortune to Combat Spirit of Militarism Now Rampant," *Detroit Journal,* 29 November 1915, p. 1.

2. "Gives $10,000 to Peace," *Providence Evening Tribune,* 23 November 1915, p. 1.

3. Laccy, *Ford: The Men and the Machine,* 147.

4. Burnet Hershey, *Odyssey of Henry Ford and the Great Peace Ship* (New York: Taplinger Publishing Company, 1950), 21.

5. Oswald Garrison Villard, *Fighting Years* (New York: Harcourt, Brace, 1939), 304.

6. "President against Ford Argosy," *Detroit Free Press,* 25 November 1915, p. 2.

7. "Great War Ends Christmas Day: Ford to Stop It," *New York Tribune,* 25 November 1915, p. 1.

8. "Editorial Opinions on Henry Ford's Peace Mission," *Detroit Free Press,* 27 November 1915, p. 3.

9. Reynold M. Wik, *Henry Ford and Grass-roots America* (Ann Arbor: University of Michigan Press, 1972), 166.

10. "Ford's Peace Ark Sails as Crowds Call Good Wishes," *New York Journal,* 6 December 1915, p. 1.

11. David L. Lewis, "The Fighting Pacifist," *Ford Life,* January–February 1973, 40.

12. "Ford Arrives Home," *Saginaw Herald,* 6 January 1916, p. 1.

CHAPTER 4

1. Lewis, *Public Image of Henry Ford,* 96. The company's war profits totaled $8,151,119.31 and when taxes had been deducted stood at $4,357,484.97. Ford's share (58.5 percent) amounted to $2,549,128.56. After deduction of personal income taxes Ford was left with profits of only $926,780.46, none of which were ever repaid to the United States Treasury.

2. Ibid.

3. Ironically enough, Ford produced Liberator bombers in Willow Run during World War II.

4. David L. Lewis, "Henry Ford in World War I," *Antique Automobile Magazine,* January–February 1974, 16.

5. Lacey, *Ford: The Men and the Machine,* 166.

6. Ibid.

7. Allan Nevins and Frank Ernest Hill, *Ford: Expansion and Challenge* (New York: Charles Scribner's Sons, 1957), 78.

8. Lewis, "Henry Ford in World War I," 18.

9. Ibid.

10. Ibid.

11. Lewis, *Public Image of Henry Ford,* 96.

12. Nevins and Hill, *Ford: Expansion and Challenge,* 118.

13. "How Ballots Stood," *Detroit Journal,* 10 June 1916, p. 2.

14. "Ford Hits Plan to Split U.S.," *Detroit News,* 4 November 1918, p. 16.

15. "Why Ford's Candidacy Is Important," advertisement, *Detroit Free Press,* 4 November 1918, p. 10.

16. Lacey, *Ford: The Men and the Machine,* 168.

17. "Vote against Ford, Soldiers' Kin Ask," *Detroit Free Press,* 3 November 1918, p. 4.

18. Theodore Roosevelt, "Editorial Letter," *Detroit Saturday Night,* 26 October 1918, p. 4.

19. "Henry Ford and His Huns," *Detroit Free Press,* 3 November 1918, p. 18.

20. "Ford Answers Hughes," *Detroit News,* 5 November 1918, p. 1.

21. Ibid.

22. "Emde Answers Ford's Critics," *Detroit News,* 5 November 1918, p. 21.

23. Lewis, *Public Image of Henry Ford,* 99.

24. The League of Nations was established as part of the Treaty of Versailles in 1919, with headquarters in Geneva, Switzerland. President Wilson was the chief planner of the League, but he could not persuade the United States to join it. The League was dissolved in April 1946, and the United Nations took its place.

CHAPTER 5

1. "As the Flivvers Roll out the Dollars Roll In," *Detroit Saturday Night,* 9 September 1922, p. 6.

2. "Henry Ford in the White House," *Detroit Saturday Night,* 11 November 1922, p. 1.

3. Ibid.

4. "The Sacrifice of Newberry," *Detroit Saturday Night,* 25 November 1922, p. 1.

5. Lewis, *Public Image of Henry Ford,* 215.

6. Maurice Hindus, "Henry Ford Conquers Russia," *Outlook,* 26 March 1924, 282.

7. "Ford First in Final Returns," *Collier's Weekly,* 14 July 1923, 5. Votes for others: McAdoo, 19,000; Borah, 3,904; Cox, 16,268; Davis, 3,317; Hoover, 9,907; Hughes, 13,761; Johnson, 14,493; La Follette, 6,963; Smith, 14,676; Underwood, 3,720; Wood, 4,116; Roosevelt, 20; Taft 15; Pershing, 15; Bryan, 138; Debs, 445; Lowden, 2,036.

8. Charles W. Wood, "If I Were President," *Collier's Weekly,* 4 August 1923, 5–6.

9. Ibid., 29.

10. "Ford Candidacy Looming Larger," *New York Times,* 18 October 1923, p. 23.

11. "Says Ford Will Get Prohibition Nomination: Chairman Summons Party to Washington," *New York Times,* 19 October 1923, p. 1.

12. "Edison Opposes Ford for President," *New York Times,* 18 October 1923, p. 23.

13. "Couzens Ridicules Ford Candidacy," *New York Times,* 1 November 1923, p. 2.

14. Louise B. Clancy and Florence Davis, *The Believer: The Life Story of Mrs. Henry Ford* (New York: Coward-McCann, 1960), 201.

CHAPTER 6

1. "Mr. Ford's Proposal for Muscle Shoals Development," *Michigan Business Farmer,* 23 July 1921, p. 1.

2. "South Is Eager to Let Shoals," *Detroit News,* 12 December 1921, p. 1.

3. Robert L. Duffus, *The Valley and Its People: A Portrait of T.V.A.* (New York: Knopf, 1944), 53, quoted in Wik, *Henry Ford and Grass-roots America,* 107.

4. Gelderman, *Henry Ford: The Wayward Capitalist*, 248.

5. "South Is Eager to Let Shoals," *Detroit News*, 12 December 1921, p. 1.

6. Ibid.

7. "Ford Challenges 'Fertilizer Trust,' " *New York Times*, 15 January 1922, p. 1.

8. "Edison Guest of Ford Today," *Detroit News*, 1 December 1922, p. 1.

9. "Bill Demands U.S. Run Shoals," *Detroit News*, 9 April 1922, p. 2.

10. Gelderman, *Henry Ford: The Wayward Capitalist*, 248–49.

11. "Ford Candidacy Looming Larger," *New York Times*, 18 October 1923, p. 23.

12. Wik, *Henry Ford and Grass-roots America*, 179.

13. Ibid.

14. "Coolidge Denies He Was to Deliver the Shoals to Ford," *New York Times*, 29 April 1924, pp. 1, 4.

15. "House Speeds up on Muscle Shoals," *New York Times*, 6 March 1924, p. 3.

16. "Couzens Ridicules Ford's Candidacy," *New York Times*, 1 November 1923, p. 2.

17. "Coolidge Denies He Was to Deliver the Shoals," p. 4.

18. "Senate Committee Calls Ford's Secretary on Telegrams at Muscle Shoals Hearing," *New York Times*, 27 April 1924, p. 1.

19. "Liebold Says Ford Never Got Message—Miller Reaffirms Statement," *New York Times*, 29 April 1924, p. 4.

20. Ibid.

21. "Coolidge Denies He Was to Deliver the Shoals," p. 4.

22. Gelderman, *Henry Ford: The Wayward Capitalist*, 249.

CHAPTER 7

1. Lacey, *Ford: The Men and the Machine*, 204–5.

2. Jonathan Norton Leonard, *The Tragedy of Henry Ford* (New York: G. P. Putnam's Sons, 1932), 186.

3. "Ford to Publish Newspaper," *Augusta Journal*, 26 November 1918, p. 1.

4. "Ford's Great Expectations," *Brooklyn Eagle*, 26 November 1918, p. 1.

5. "Today: Henry Ford, Publisher," *Detroit Times*, 23 November 1918, p. 1.

6. Lacey, *Ford: The Men and the Machine*, 205.

7. "Our International Weekly," *Detroit Saturday Night*, 18 January 1919, p. 9.

8. Lewis, *Public Image of Henry Ford*, 137.

9. J. J. O'Neill to E. G. Liebold, 26 November 1919, accession 62, box 81, Henry Ford Museum and Greenfield Village Research Library, Dearborn, MI.

10. Ibid.

11. "The International Jew: The World's Problem," *Dearborn Independent*, 22 May 1920, p. 1.

12. Ibid.

13. Gelderman, *Henry Ford: The Wayward Capitalist*, 220.

14. Ibid.

15. "Does a Jewish World Program Exist?" *Dearborn Independent*, 10 April 1920, p. 5.

16. Rabbi Franklin, "Rabbi Lauds Ford for His Apology," *Detroit Times*, 9 July 1927, p. 26.

17. "How the Jewish Question Touches the Farm," *Dearborn Independent*, 4 September 1920, p. 8.

18. Henry Ford, *My Life and Work* (New York: Doubleday, Page, 1922), 250.

19. "Jewish Exploitation of Farmer Organization," *Dearborn Independent*, 12 April 1924, p. 3.

20. "Sapiro's Farm Studies Told," *Detroit News*, 29 March 1929, p. 1.

21. Gelderman, *Henry Ford: The Wayward Capitalist*, 227–28.

22. Lacy, *Ford: The Men and the Machine*, 226.

23. "What Raymond Says of Mistrial Verdict," *Detroit Times*, 22 April 1927, p. 2.

24. Ibid.

25. Ibid.

26. Ibid.

27. "Mr. Ford's Statement," *Detroit News*, 8 July 1927, p. 1.

28. Lewis, *Public Image of Henry Ford*, 146.

29. Franklin, "Rabbi Lauds Ford," p. 26.

30. "Julius Rosenwald Says Jews Ready to Forgive," *Christian Science Monitor*, 8 July 1927, sec. A, p. A4, Atlantic edition.

31. "Assert Ford Acted Alone on Apology," *New York Times,* 10 July 1927, p. 18.

32. "Sapiro Will Settle Suit," *Ann Arbor Times News,* 11 July 1927, p. 1.

Chapter 8

1. Gelderman, *Henry Ford: The Wayward Capitalist,* 254.

2. Ibid., 258–59.

3. Ibid., 259.

4. Ralph Z. Thatcher, "Have You a Case of Ford-osis, Too?" *Detroit News,* 28 January 1928, p. 2.

5. Nevins and Hill, *Ford: The Times, The Man, The Company,* 455.

6. Lewis, *Public Image of Henry Ford,* 203.

7. Ibid., 203–4.

8. Ibid., 205.

9. Thatcher, "Have You a Case of Ford-osis, Too?"

Chapter 9

1. Ford Motor Company Archives, "The Reminiscences of Mr. John Williams" (Detroit: Ford Motor Company Oral History Section, 1954), 17.

2. David E. Nye, *Henry Ford: Ignorant Idealist* (New York: Kennikat Press, 1979), 112.

3. Lorin Sorensen, *The Ford Road* (California: Silverado Publishing, 1978), 63.

4. Ford Motor Company Archives, "Reminiscences of Mr. Fred Black" (Detroit: Ford Motor Company Oral Historical Section, 1953), 158.

Index

Italicized page numbers signify that information is located within the caption of an illustration.